The Alcohol Recovery Ally

SUPPORTIVE TOOLS FOR THE SOBRIETY JOURNEY

MONICA CROSS

MONICA CROSS

Method Attribution & Usage Rights

The Shadowframe Method™, the Freeze-Frame Strategy™, and the Recovery Ally Model™ are original concepts developed by Monica Cross to support addiction recovery, self-reflection, and effective communication. These methods may be freely used by individuals, educators, and recovery professionals, provided that proper credit is given to the original creator.

Fair Use & Limitations

While this book is intended to educate and support recovery efforts, it does not grant permission for commercial reproduction, adaptation, or rebranding of these methods under another name. Any public or professional use should acknowledge the source as:

Monica Cross, creator of the Shadowframe Method™, the Freeze-Frame Strategy™, and the Recovery Ally Model™.

Trademark Claim

The terms The Shadowframe Method™, The Freeze-Frame Strategy™, and The Recovery Ally Model™ are claimed trademarks of Monica Cross. Their use in professional training, certification programs, or commercial applications requires direct permission from the author.

Disclaimer

This book is not a substitute for professional medical, psychological, or addiction counseling. The techniques described herein are meant to complement, not replace, professional treatment. Readers should consult a qualified healthcare provider for medical or psychological advice.

Alcohol Use Disorder (AUD) and related concerns are complex medical conditions that require individualized evaluation and care from trained professionals. If you or someone you know is struggling with alcohol use, it is strongly recommended that you seek guidance from a licensed healthcare provider, addiction specialist, or mental health professional.

Additionally, this book is not a replacement for structured support groups, recovery programs, or professional counseling. While the insights provided may be helpful in understanding AUD, sustainable recovery often benefits from community support, therapy, or programs such as SMART Recovery, Alcoholics Anonymous (AA), or other evidence-based recovery models.

The author disclaims any liability for decisions made based on the information in this book. Consumers of this book assume full responsibility for how they choose to apply the concepts discussed herein. If you are encountering a medical or mental health crisis, please seek immediate help from a medical professional or emergency services.

Dedication

For you, the reader—whether you are walking the path of recovery, standing beside someone who is, guiding others through their journey, or simply seeking to understand. This book exists because of you.

Your efforts matter. Your courage matters.

You matter.

Contents

Preface

Recently, I learned of a member of my community who lost his battle with addiction. Nothing could ever fully describe the pain on his father's face as he grappled with his loss. I found myself struggling to understand how the despair of addiction could drive someone to end their own life.

This moment—along with many other personal stories—was the reason I began this journey. The knowledge and insights I've gained along the way are now encapsulated in this book.

Since starting this journey, I've become certified to facilitate recovery groups, hoping to support those in need. That course opened the proverbial can of worms for me. I realized that there were so many topics that I needed to research before I could ever feel confident enough to run a group, no matter how structured they are designed to be. I read what feels like countless books, searching for answers. Still, every time I finished one book, it led me to another topic that I needed to explore. I am not done learning—but are any of us ever truly done?

During a conversation with a friend who has struggled with Alcohol Use Disorder (AUD), his parting words stuck with me: "I hope you can help someone." His words made me realize that I needed to share what I've learned, even if it isn't perfect. And so, this book—one I never intended to write—began to take shape.

There's an old saying that "a little knowledge is a dangerous thing." The truth, though, is that too much knowledge can be overwhelming. All of that new information became like the pieces of a jigsaw puzzle that were finally starting to flow into place. I needed to write this book. I needed to find a way to put words to ideas that were too much to convey in any other form. This book assembles the loose threads of my research and weaves them together with my thoughts to form the fabric of words on the pages.

The title of this book introduces the Recovery Ally™. As the reader progresses through the book, they may begin to see that a Recovery Ally is more than the model presented in Chapter 5. The Shadowframe Method™ is a tool that I created after reading an ACT book, and it was a powerful tool when I got the "feeling" right. The Freeze-Frame Scenarios™ are a teaching tool aligned with adult learning theory. They are designed to shift one's perspective and are rooted in the ethical principle that planning ahead can support making the best decision when a situation arises.

Before deciding to write this book—admittedly with some support from AI—I came to an important realization: many people struggling with addiction and recovery may not have the time, energy, or ability to sift through all the complex research and literature on AUD.

That's why this book exists. It distills and synthesizes a wide range of evidence-based insights, making vital information accessible in a single resource. As I searched for something similar in the publishing marketplace, I found nothing quite like what I envisioned. So, despite knowing it may never feel as comprehensive or perfectly organized as I'd like, I knew I had to get it into the hands of anyone who might find that it strengthens their journey to lasting sobriety.

As stated in my disclaimer, this book is not medical advice nor a substitute for professional help. My background is in education, not psychology. I'm a whole-to-parts thinker—I gather information, analyze it, and form new connections. When these insights came together, I turned to AI tools to help organize them into something readable and accessible for anyone who picks up this book.

I believe that evidence-based information and support for those affected by Alcohol Use Disorder should be available to everyone who seeks it. My hope is that this book serves that purpose.

CHAPTER ONE

Introduction

Addiction to alcohol has nothing to do with character. Alcohol Use Disorder (AUD) develops when the body adapts to repeated and prolonged exposure to a toxic substance, gradually becoming dependent on it. Over time, the physical, chemical, and emotional toll builds until both the body and brain become enslaved by its use.

Culturally, alcohol is widely accepted, and often associated with freedom, fun, and social connection. However, what may start as casual drinking can quickly turn into a substitute for genuine solutions—ultimately replacing the true freedoms that come with a sober life.

The Alcohol Recovery Ally: Supportive Tools for the Sobriety Journey is designed for anyone involved in the recovery process. It supports individuals in recovery, sponsors, and group facilitators in taking an active and ongoing role in sobriety. It is also suitable for use in recovery groups, including those welcoming individuals who have not yet made the decision to stop drinking.

This book provides a versatile toolkit of science-backed therapy methods, including Motivational Interviewing (MI), Cognitive Behavioral Therapy (CBT), Dialectical Behavior Therapy (DBT), and Acceptance and Commitment Therapy (ACT). The tools and prompts included help deepen understanding, enhance self-efficacy, and strengthen coping skills in recovery. A wide range of MI prompts are provided to help individuals clarify their relationship with alcohol and develop strategies for making meaningful changes.

Recovery from AUD is challenging. Anxiety, work stress, loneliness, relationship struggles, depression, and trauma are just a few of the pressures that frequently contribute to relapse. This book is designed to support the ongoing renewal of commitment to sobriety by helping individuals anticipate obstacles, explore solutions, and navigate crises. The MI prompts can be adapted for discussions, journaling, and self-exploration.

While therapists and group facilitators may find this guide useful, it is equally accessible to individuals with little to no prior knowledge of the recovery process. The book is designed to be flexible—it does not need to be read in order, from cover to cover. Instead, readers are encouraged to engage with the material in a way that best meets their personal needs.

There are no rigid rules for using this guide. Readers should feel free to rephrase, adapt, and tailor the tools and prompts to fit their unique circumstances. When used flexibly and consistently, this book can serve as a practical, enduring resource throughout the recovery journey.

CHAPTER TWO

The Journey To Sobriety

UNDERSTANDING ALCOHOL WITHDRAWAL AND RECOVERY

Choosing to become sober is a life-changing decision that requires careful consideration and often professional guidance. This chapter provides a comprehensive overview of the alcohol withdrawal process, the journey to recovery, and the concerning condition called kindling.

The Decision to Get Sober

The decision to stop drinking is deeply personal and often stems from various factors, including health concerns, relationship issues, legal problems, financial difficulties, and personal growth aspirations. It's crucial to understand that while not everyone will experience severe withdrawal symptoms, abruptly stopping alcohol consumption can be dangerous for some individuals, especially heavy drinkers or those with a long history of alcohol use.

Alcohol Withdrawal Syndrome (AWS)

Alcohol Withdrawal Syndrome is a set of symptoms that can occur following a reduction in alcohol use after a period of excessive consumption. The severity of withdrawal can vary from mild symptoms to severe and life-threatening conditions.

Factors Affecting Withdrawal Severity

Deciding to quit drinking is a courageous step, but alcohol withdrawal is not just uncomfortable—it can be life-threatening. The severity of symptoms depends on several factors, including:

- Duration and amount of alcohol use
- Overall health and age
- Previous withdrawal experiences
- Co-occurring mental health conditions

For individuals with a history of heavy or prolonged alcohol use, medical supervision during detox is critical, as withdrawal can lead to seizures, heart complications, or even death.

Alcohol Withdrawal Timeline

While experiences vary, the general progression of alcohol withdrawal follows this timeline:

First 6-12 Hours After Last Drink

- Anxiety, restlessness, nausea
  - Mild tremors, headache, insomnia

12-24 Hours

- Worsening tremors, increased anxiety, irritability
  - Disorientation or difficulty concentrating
  - In some cases, hallucinations (visual, auditory, or tactile)

24-72 Hours (Peak Withdrawal Period – Highest Risk of Severe Complications) *

- Seizure risk increases significantly
  - Elevated blood pressure and heart rate
  - Excessive sweating and confusion
  - Delirium Tremens (DTs) may develop in 5-15% of cases, leading to:
    - Severe agitation
    - Fever and heavy sweating
    - Hallucinations
    - Dangerous fluctuations in heart rate and blood pressure
    - Seizures that can lead to fatal complications.

* This 24-72 hour stage of withdrawal is the most dangerous period. Withdrawal-related deaths most commonly occur within this peak withdrawal period, especially if DTs develop without medical intervention.

72 Hours to 7 Days

● For most individuals, symptoms begin improving, but some may experience lingering effects

　　● Physical withdrawal symptoms generally subside

　　● Psychological symptoms (such as anxiety, depression, or mood swings) may persist

Week 2 and Beyond: The Long-Term Recovery Phase

● Most acute withdrawal symptoms fade, but some individuals develop Post-Acute Withdrawal Syndrome (PAWS).

　　● PAWS can include fatigue, mood swings, brain fog, and intense cravings that persist for weeks or months.

　　● Many people report that cravings temporarily subside, only to return around 3-6 months into sobriety—a critical period that can lead to relapse if unprepared.

The Kindling Effect

Some individuals who undergo repeated withdrawal episodes face worsening withdrawal symptoms over time. This is known as the kindling effect. Several factors influence whether someone will experience progressively worse withdrawal symptoms, including:

　　● **The more times a person detoxes from alcohol, the higher the likelihood of kindling.**

• Heavy, long-term drinkers are more prone to kindling than those with shorter histories of alcohol dependence.

• Some individuals may have a greater predisposition to kindling due to underlying brain chemistry.

• Co-occurring mental health issues, such as anxiety or PTSD, can amplify withdrawal severity, increasing the risk of kindling.

While not everyone who experiences multiple withdrawals will suffer from kindling, the risk increases with repeated detox attempts. This is why medical detox is strongly recommended for individuals with a history of severe withdrawal symptoms, particularly those who have previously experienced seizures or delirium tremens (DTs).

Why Medical Supervision is Essential

While some people experience only mild withdrawal symptoms, there is no way to predict exactly how withdrawal will unfold—even for those who have quit drinking before. Some may believe they can detox alone, but without medical care, they risk the possibility of seizures, heart complications, and delirium tremens, the latter of which can be deadly without medical treatment.

Supervised medical detox provides medication-assisted withdrawal to reduce seizure risk and ease symptoms, monitoring of vital signs to prevent life-threatening complications, and follow-up emotional support and relapse prevention strategies for long-term recovery

Alcohol withdrawal is a serious medical condition—one that deserves proper care. The safest approach is a medically supervised detox, especially for those with a history of heavy drinking, previous withdrawal episodes, or underlying health issues.

For those considering sobriety: Talk to a doctor, seek professional support, and don't try to do it alone. Recovery is possible—and it starts with a safe detox.

CHAPTER THREE

Understanding Alcohol's Impact

BEYOND THE MYTHS

Alcohol consumption is deeply ingrained in many cultures, often portrayed as a harmless social lubricant. Research has long suggested that moderate drinking—defined as up to one drink per day for women and two for men—carries little risk, and some studies have even suggested potential health benefits, such as improved heart health. However, newer research challenges these assumptions, revealing that even moderate drinking can negatively impact sleep, emotions, and physical health over time.

Alcohol and Sleep Disruption

Many people believe alcohol helps them sleep better, but the opposite is true. While alcohol might make you feel drowsy, it disrupts the natural sleep cycle, reducing the quality of rest. It prevents deep, restorative sleep and increases the likelihood of waking up throughout the night. Over time, poor sleep affects cognitive function, emotional stability, and overall physical health, contributing to issues such as anxiety, depression, and weakened immune function.

Emotional and Physical Health Consequences

Alcohol has a complex relationship with emotions. Initially, it may create feelings of relaxation and euphoria, but as its effects wear off, it can contribute to increased anxiety, mood swings, and even depression. The body adapts to alcohol consumption by altering neurotransmitter activity, which can make individuals more prone to negative emotions over time.

Physically, alcohol affects nearly every organ system. It raises blood pressure, taxes the liver, and contributes to inflammation throughout the body. Long-term use increases the risk of cardiovascular disease, certain cancers, and digestive issues. Additionally, alcohol inhibits the absorption of essential nutrients, including those crucial for vegetarians and vegans, exacerbating deficiencies and overall health problems.

The Subtle Progression of Alcohol Dependence

Alcohol use often starts innocently—at social gatherings, celebrations, or as a way to unwind. However, the body gradually builds a tolerance, requiring more alcohol to achieve the same effects. This subtle progression can lead to dependence before individuals even realize it. Over time, drinking can become a central part of daily life, interfering with relationships, work, and personal values.

Societal Influences and Normalization

Society normalizes alcohol consumption in ways that mask its potential dangers. Marketing campaigns highlight its role in relaxation and fun. Social events often revolve around drinking. The distinction between a "casual drinker" and an "alcoholic" creates a false binary, making it seem as though problems only exist at the extremes. In reality, alcohol affects everyone differently, and even moderate use carries risks.

Debunking Myths About "Harmless" Drinking

~~Myth: A glass of wine a day is good for the heart.~~
    Reality: While some studies have suggested benefits, newer research indicates that any amount of alcohol increases the risk of heart disease and other health problems.
    ~~Myth: Drinking helps you sleep.~~
    Reality: Alcohol disrupts REM sleep, leading to fatigue and cognitive impairment over time.
    ~~Myth: Only alcoholics experience withdrawal symptoms.~~
    Reality: Even casual drinkers can experience mild withdrawal, including anxiety, irritability, and poor sleep, as the body adjusts to alcohol's absence.

~~Myth: Alcohol is harmless as long as you drink in moderation.~~

Reality: Emerging evidence suggests that no amount of alcohol is truly risk-free, particularly regarding cancer, brain health, and long-term emotional well-being.

Understanding the true effects of alcohol requires looking past societal norms and marketing messages. While moderate drinking may not seem harmful, research continues to reveal its risks, particularly in how it disrupts sleep, alters emotions, and affects physical health. By challenging common myths and recognizing the gradual progression toward dependence, individuals can make more informed choices about alcohol use.

Moving Forward

Recovery isn't about perfection—it's about progress. Remember:

- Small steps lead to big changes.

- Cravings are temporary and manageable.

- Changing thoughts can change behavior.

- Changing behaviors can change thoughts.

- A healthy lifestyle supports long-term success.

If you're struggling, seek support. There are many paths to recovery—therapy, peer groups, and self-help resources. The most important thing is to keep going. You have the power to change. Take it one step at a time.

CHAPTER FOUR

Building A Strong Foundation For Lasting Sobriety

Getting sober is the first step. Staying sober takes effort. Long term recovery goes beyond avoiding alcohol. It is about creating a life where sobriety feels natural. That means taking care of your body and mind, surrounding yourself with the right people, and building the skills to handle whatever life throws your way. A strong foundation does not happen overnight, but with the right approach, it can support a lifetime of recovery.

Strengthening Physical and Mental Health

Your health plays a huge role in recovery, and there is no single path that works for everyone. Some people choose medical treatment, including supervised detox or medication assisted treatment. Others focus on structured routines, better nutrition, and movement to rebuild their strength. What matters is finding what works for you and supports long term stability.

Exercise is more than a way to improve your mood. It helps regulate stress, restores the body's ability to function well, and improves sleep. Moving your body, whether it is stretching, walking, or engaging in an activity that feels right, can help create a sense of control.

Mental health is just as important. Therapy can be a powerful tool, but it is not the only one. Free resources, support groups, and self reflection through journaling or other structured exercises can also help. Structured exercises can help guide meaningful reflection and strengthen self-awareness. Later in this book, you will be introduced to tools like Motivational Interviewing prompts and Freeze-Frame activities, which can be useful for this purpose, whether used alone or with a Recovery Ally. Recognizing patterns and understanding what fuels cravings or strengthens your resolve can help you stay on track.

Creating a Life That Supports Sobriety

Recovery is not just about quitting drinking—it is about building something better. The people around you make a difference. Whether it is Alcoholics Anonymous, SMART Recovery, or trusted friends and family, having a support system helps shift the focus from what you are leaving behind to what you are creating.

Structure and routine can help. When your days have purpose, staying on track becomes easier. Work, hobbies, and meaningful activities provide stability. Stress, boredom, and old habits can make drinking feel like an option, but having strategies in place helps. Some people step outside, shift focus, or engage in activities that require concentration. Deep breathing or observing your surroundings works for some, while others need action based solutions like working with their hands, playing music, or reaching out to someone who understands. The key is finding what works for you.

Navigating Challenges and Staying Committed

Relapse can seem sudden, but it is often influenced by underlying stress, exhaustion, or isolation that has been building over time. It builds over time, often through stress, exhaustion, or isolation. Knowing your personal triggers makes it easier to manage tough situations before they escalate. When cravings hit, it is not always about resisting—it is about redirecting. Calling a support person, stepping away from a situation, or physically moving to a new space can help break the cycle. Writing down your reasons for staying sober or having a list of quick actions to take can be a lifeline in difficult moments.

Recovery is about more than just avoiding alcohol. It is about setting goals, finding purpose, and reinforcing the decision to live sober. Some days will be harder than others, but learning from challenges, staying connected, and having a plan makes the path forward clearer.

Looking Ahead

Sobriety is a lifelong process, and having the right support system makes all the difference. The next chapter focuses on The Recovery Ally. It explores the role of loved ones in providing encouragement and accountability in recovery.

CHAPTER FIVE

The Recovery Ally ™

A PROPOSED PEER SUPPORT ROLE

While structured recovery programs provide essential tools and group support, individual group participants may benefit from a trusted Recovery Ally who can provide personalized encouragement and accountability. The concept of a Recovery Ally is a peer support role that is complementary to existing recovery frameworks. The Recovery Ally offers individualized, skills-based support outside of formal meetings. This role is not intended to replace professional therapy, structured recovery programs, or medical intervention, but rather to serve as an additional layer of peer-driven encouragement and reinforcement.

The Role Of A Recovery Ally

A Recovery Ally can be a friend, peer, or coach who is trained in, or committed to using, Motivational Interviewing (MI) techniques to support someone in their long-term recovery journey. Unlike traditional sponsorship models, the Recovery Ally would focus on empowerment through coaching dialogue that promotes skill-building, accountability, and independence. Even in the absence of formal MI training, a Recovery Ally could provide meaningful support through active listening and structured engagement.

Core Principles of the Recovery Ally Concept

Encouraging Autonomy: The role is meant to guide, not dictate, allowing participants to make their own decisions.

Skill-Based Reinforcement: Recovery Allies focus on strengthening key recovery tools, such as Cost-Benefit Analysis (CBA), the ABC Framework, and strategies for managing urges and cravings.

Accountability Partnership: Regular check-ins and structured conversations help participants stay on track with their goals.

Strength-Based Approach: The focus remains on leveraging the participant's personal strengths and resilience.

Flexible Methodology: Recovery Allies may incorporate approaches from various therapeutic disciplines, such as CBT, DBT, ACT, and MI, to best support each individual.

Potential Responsibilities of a Recovery Ally

Regular Check-Ins: Scheduled conversations, in-person or virtual, to discuss progress and challenges.

Application of Recovery Tools: Encouraging the practical use of frameworks such as CBA and ABC Worksheets in real-life situations.

Crisis Support: Providing real-time encouragement and reinforcing distress tolerance techniques.

Motivational Reinforcement: Using MI principles to help participants navigate ambivalence and sustain intrinsic motivation.

Constructive Feedback: Encouraging reflection on setbacks as learning opportunities.

Helpful Skills For The Recovery Ally To Possess

While the role of a Recovery Ally would be informal and voluntary, certain skills and understandings could enhance its effectiveness. These valuable skills include:

- Familiarity with addiction and recovery principles.

- Understanding of strategies and tools used in 4-Points programs, like SMART Recovery.

- Awareness of adult learning and coaching techniques.

- Ability to maintain clear boundaries and uphold participant empowerment.

- Active listening skills and adherence to MI questioning techniques.

- Commitment to fostering accountability and goal-oriented

dialogue.

Establishing a Recovery Ally Partnership

- *Implementation:* A Recovery Ally partnership permits a structured yet adaptable format:

- *Initial Matching:* Participants identify their preferred communication styles and recovery goals, seeking allies who align with their needs.

- *First Meeting:* Expectations and boundaries are agreed upon, and accountability tools & goal-setting are introduced as a topic for upcoming meetings.

Ongoing and Evolving Supports:

- Weekly check-ins for structured discussions.

- Crisis support within predetermined boundaries.

- Periodic review of tool application and skill development.

- As participants progress, participants and allies continually assess the value of the partnership and determine when or how to pivot strategies or to transition out of the role.

Suggested Recovery Ally Toolkit

There are many tools that a Recovery Ally can access to assist in assembling a personalized toolkit for sobriety. Because recovery is personal, ongoing, and constantly evolving, the individualized toolkit may include meaningful work that has been generated in group recovery meetings and therapy sessions, or even from this book. Some beneficial tasks and products might include:

- *Action Plan Template:* A structured plan for setting and achieving recovery goals.

- *Crisis Response Cards:* A quick-reference guide for managing high-risk situations.

- *Progress and Urge Trackers:* Logs for monitoring achievements & obstacles, and urges, cravings, and triggers.

- *ABC Worksheets:* A tool for reframing challenging situations, such as those documented in an Urge Log.

- *Motivational Scripts:* Exercises and reminders for reinforcing commitment to change.

- *Evocative Shadowframe Image:* Digital or paper copy that can be viewed immediately when an urge or craving is triggered.

How a Recovery Ally Can Enhance the Recovery Journey

• *Pre-Meeting Preparation:* Helping newcomers feel more confident in recovery settings.

　　• *Between-Meeting Reinforcement:* Offering continuity and support beyond formal group sessions.

　　• *Relapse Prevention:* Providing early intervention by recognizing and addressing warning signs.

Potential Impacts from The Recovery Ally Model

Although the Recovery Ally concept has not yet been tested as an evidence-based practice, it represents another avenue for enhancing peer support within recovery frameworks. With care, this approach could:

- *Enhance Recovery Engagement*: Providing additional motivation and consistency in the recovery journey.

- *Encourage Practical Skill Application*: Reinforcing the use of recovery tools in daily life.

- *Build Community Support*: Strengthening peer relationships and fostering shared growth.

- *Promote Leadership and Empowerment*: Encouraging individuals in recovery to give back and support others.

The Process of Recovery: A Lifelong Journey of Growth

Recovery is not a single event but an ongoing process that demands commitment, self-reflection, and adaptability. Each stage presents new challenges and insights, offering opportunities for personal growth and self-discovery. Understanding the evolving nature of recovery can help reinforce your resilience and long-term success.

CHAPTER SIX

It's Never One And Done

IT'S A JOURNEY

It's called spiraling. It's an educational tool that intentionally revisits previously taught content. With each new pass through, new information is added in with the old. This is not unlike layers of an onion. When you peel back one layer, there is another one waiting to be peeled back next. That's how learning works. Learning takes place through repetition. New understandings evolve from change. New understandings prepare us for deeper knowledge. We need time to take in knowledge in digestible amounts. This chapter is part of the spiral. It's never one and done. There's always another layer.

Understanding Alcohol's Grip and Reclaiming Your Life

For many, alcohol serves as both a coping mechanism and an adversary—offering temporary relief while silently undermining health, relationships, and personal aspirations. Breaking free requires a deep understanding of its impact. Alcohol disrupts brain chemistry, impairing decision-making, impulse control, and emotional regulation. It rewires the brain's reward system, making cravings feel overpowering, and contributes to mental health struggles, including anxiety and depression. Over time, its physical toll increases the risk of liver disease, cardiovascular problems, and sleep disturbances.

Sustained sobriety requires identifying the emotional and environmental cues that once fueled drinking habits. Triggers can include stress, loneliness, social anxiety, or boredom, and patterns may emerge when reflecting on when, where, and why alcohol was used. Many drink to escape pain, numb emotions, or boost confidence, creating an emotional dependency that reinforces the habit. Recognizing these patterns is crucial to breaking free.

Reflecting on alcohol's impact reinforces the decision to stay sober. Relationships suffer, trust is lost, and important moments with loved ones slip away. Goals, whether personal, professional, or educational, are often delayed or derailed. Financial consequences accumulate, from the direct costs of alcohol to medical and legal expenses. Over time, alcohol also shapes self-perception, influencing confidence, self-worth, and identity.

Even after years of sobriety, the mind can rationalize drinking again. Thought distortions make relapse seem justifiable: believing that "just one drink won't hurt," convincing oneself that "control is possible," or minimizing past struggles by glamorizing old experiences. The brain never fully resets its response to alcohol. Neurological pathways formed during addiction remain, making relapse a significant risk—even after years of sobriety. Before taking that first drink, it's important to pause and ask whether alcohol ever truly worked as a form of moderation. Has it ever been sustainable? Is one moment of indulgence worth risking years of progress? Seeking support in these moments can be the difference between staying on track and falling back into old patterns. Talking to a therapist or sponsor, reflecting on past struggles with moderation, and remembering that addiction is a neurological condition—not a failure of willpower—are powerful tools for staying committed.

Your reasons for staying sober are powerful. They serve as reminders of why you chose this path and keep you motivated when challenges arise. A sober life brings more energy, better health, stronger relationships, financial savings, and a clearer mind. Setting goals for the future creates purpose—what does life without alcohol look like? What dreams have been put on hold? Breaking big goals into smaller steps makes them more manageable and keeps progress in focus. It also helps to remember what alcohol took away. Writing down difficult moments, tracking personal progress, and keeping reminders of why sobriety matters can provide strength in moments of doubt.

There will be times when the urge to drink resurfaces. Recognizing triggers—certain people, places, situations, stress, boredom, celebrations, or even memories—allows for better preparation. Cravings can be managed by engaging in deep breathing, reaching out to a support person, or using distractions such as listening to music, reading, or exercising. Preparing responses in advance for social situations where alcohol is present builds confidence and reinforces commitment.

Sobriety is about more than just avoiding alcohol—it's about strengthening the mind. Negative thoughts can challenge progress, but they can also be reframed. "I'll never be able to do this" becomes "I've made it this far, and I'm getting stronger every day." "One drink won't hurt" shifts to "Will this choice help or hurt my progress?" Processing emotions in healthy ways—journaling, talking to a trusted friend, or engaging in creative outlets—supports long-term recovery. Setting small, achievable goals, such as practicing gratitude, spending time with supportive people, or taking a few minutes to breathe and reflect, reinforces a positive mindset.

A fulfilling, alcohol-free life is built on balance, resilience, and joy. Making time for what brings happiness, learning to say no to stressors, and exploring new or forgotten passions make sobriety sustainable. At times, challenges will arise, but focusing on what can be controlled, practicing mindfulness, and letting go of perfection allow for growth. Setbacks do not define recovery—they offer opportunities to strengthen it.

Practicing gratitude shifts perspective and reinforces commitment. Writing down three things to be thankful for, noticing small moments of joy, and expressing appreciation to those who support the journey can make a profound difference. Recovery is not a straight path, and there is no single way forward. Progress happens in small steps, and each decision to stay sober builds a stronger foundation for the future. Every day of sobriety is worth celebrating, and every challenge overcome is a reminder of the strength within.

How Alcohol Alters the Brain and Body

- **Disrupts brain chemistry,** impairing decision-making, impulse control, and emotional regulation.
- **Rewires the brain's reward system,** making cravings feel overpowering.
- **Contributes to mental health struggles, including anxiety and depression.**
- **Affects physical health,** increasing the risk of liver disease, cardiovascular problems, and sleep disturbances.

Recognizing Patterns and Triggers

Sustained sobriety requires identifying the emotional and environmental cues that once fueled drinking habits:

- **Pinpoint personal triggers**—stress, loneliness, social anxiety, boredom.
- **Analyze past drinking habits**—when, where, and why alcohol was used.
- **Recognize emotional dependencies**—drinking to escape, numb pain, or boost confidence.

Acknowledging the Consequences of Alcohol Use

- **Relationships**—strained friendships, lost trust, and missed family moments.
- **Unfulfilled goals**—delayed or derailed personal, professional, or educational aspirations.
- **Financial toll**—expenses tied to drinking, including medical and legal consequences.
- **Changes in self-perception**—how alcohol influenced confidence, self-worth, and identity.

Recognizing Thought Distortions That Lead to Relapse

Even after years of sobriety, the mind can rationalize drinking again. These cognitive distortions are dangerous:

- **"Just one drink won't hurt."** (Ignoring the brain's reinforced pathways.)

- **"I can control it now."** (Minimizing past struggles.)

- **"Drinking wasn't that bad."** (Glamorizing past experiences while ignoring negative effects.)

- **"I deserve to celebrate with a drink."** (Associating alcohol with reward and pleasure.

Challenging these thoughts in real-time is crucial to maintaining sobriety.

The Risk Isn't Worth It: Why "Just One Drink" Is a Dangerous Myth

Many in long-term recovery experience the temptation to test moderation. Whether for a special occasion, nostalgia, or a sense of control, the thought of "just one drink" can be deceiving. However, research and lived experiences reveal that the brain never fully resets its response to alcohol. Neurological pathways formed during addiction remain, making relapse a significant risk—even after years of sobriety.

Before taking that first drink, consider:

- *How has alcohol affected your life in the past?*
  - *Has moderation ever worked for you before?*
  - *Are you willing to risk undoing years of progress?*
  - *Is one moment of indulgence worth reawakening old cravings?*

For those struggling with these thoughts, seeking support before making a decision is crucial:

- Speak with a therapist or sponsor.

- Reflect on past struggles with moderation.

- Remind yourself that addiction is a neurological condition, not a failure of willpower.

Long-term sobriety is built on consistent choices. Choosing abstinence, even in moments of doubt, is the safest and most empowering path forward.

Finding Your Reasons to Stay Sober

Your reasons for staying sober are powerful. They keep you going when challenges arise, and they remind you why you chose this path.

Start by listing the benefits of sobriety:

- More energy and better health

- Stronger relationships with friends and family

- Financial savings

- A clearer mind and personal growth

Think about your future and set goals:

- What do you want your life to look like without alcohol?

- What dreams have you put on hold?

- Break big goals into smaller steps to keep them manageable.

- Check in on your progress and adjust as needed.

It also helps to remember what alcohol took from you. Over time, it's easy to forget the struggles. Keeping reminders can help you stay motivated:

- Write down difficult moments from your past.

- Keep notes about your progress and successes.

- Save reminders of your "why" to revisit on tough days.

Recovery isn't just about quitting alcohol—it's about building a life that makes you excited to stay sober.

Handling Triggers, Cravings, and Urges

There will be moments when the urge to drink hits. Understanding your triggers can help you stay in control.

Common triggers include:

- Certain people, places, or situations

- Stress, loneliness, or boredom

- Celebrations or social events

- Memories of drinking in the past

Pay attention to early warning signs like restlessness, tension, or feeling overwhelmed.

If you know your triggers, you can create a plan for handling them.

When cravings hit, try:

- Deep breathing or meditation

- Calling a friend or support person

- Keeping your hands and mouth busy with snacks, gum, or a fidget object

- Repeating positive affirmations like, "This craving will pass."

Distraction can also be a great tool. Engage in activities that keep your mind occupied, such as:

- Listening to music or a podcast

- Reading, writing, or doing a puzzle

- Exercising, even if it's just a short walk

Develop skills to say "no" to alcohol.

- Rehearse responses for when someone offers you a drink.

- Hold a non-alcoholic beverage at social events.

- Make an exit plan for uncomfortable situations.

The more you prepare, the more confident you'll feel when cravings arise.

Building a Healthy Mindset

Sobriety isn't just about avoiding alcohol—it's about strengthening your mind. Your thoughts shape your experience, so it's important to challenge negativity.

Watch for unhelpful thinking patterns and challenge them.

"I'll never be able to do this."
→ Instead, remind yourself: *"I've made it this far, and I'm getting stronger every day."*

"One drink won't hurt."
→ Instead, ask yourself: *"Will this choice help or hurt my progress?"*

If emotions feel overwhelming, find healthy ways to process them:

- Journaling can help untangle your thoughts.

- Talking to a trusted friend or counselor can provide relief.

- Activities like art, music, or movement can express feelings that are hard to put into words.

Building a healthy mindset also means setting small, achievable goals. **Start with daily or weekly intentions, such as:**

- Practicing gratitude each morning

- Spending time with supportive people

- Taking a few minutes to relax and breathe

- Every small step forward adds up.

Build Balance and Strength in Recovery

- Balance work, rest, and fun. Make time for things that bring you joy.

- Learn to say no to stressors that don't serve you.

- Explore new hobbies or revisit old ones that make you feel alive.

A fulfilling, alcohol-free life isn't just about avoiding drinking — it's about creating a life you love. At times, you may feel stuck on things you can't control. Practicing acceptance can help. Try:

- Focusing on what you *can* change instead of what you can't.

- Using mindfulness techniques to stay present.

- Letting go of perfection—progress is what matters.

- Resilience comes from learning and growing through challenges. If you have setbacks, don't let them define you. Instead, see them as chances to strengthen your recovery.

Finally, practicing gratitude can shift your mindset in a powerful way. Each day, try to:

- Write down three things you're thankful for.

- Notice small moments of joy, like a kind word or a beautiful sunset.

- Express appreciation to those who support you.

Recovery is a journey, and there's no single path that fits everyone. Be patient with yourself as you navigate the ups and downs, knowing that growth takes time. Celebrate your progress—big or small—and lean on your support system when challenges arise. The more you practice these strategies, the more natural they will feel, becoming part of your everyday life. Stay committed, keep learning, and trust in your own strength. Every day you choose sobriety is a step toward a healthier, more fulfilling future—and that's always worth celebrating.

CHAPTER SEVEN

Strategies To Build Resilience

Recovery takes more than resisting cravings with willpower. It requires strategies that help you navigate challenges and stay in control. Cravings and emotional triggers do not disappear overnight. Without the right tools, it is easy to feel overwhelmed or stuck in old habits.

The strategies here focus on different aspects of recovery. They help manage intrusive thoughts, build healthier behaviors, and strengthen emotional resilience. Using these tools makes it easier to handle cravings and stay on track. Long-term recovery becomes possible when you have a plan that works.

Cognitive Strategies

- **Cognitive restructuring:** Challenge and reframe irrational thoughts that fuel cravings.

- **Mindfulness practice:** Stay present and observe cravings without judgment.

- **Urge surfing:** Visualize cravings as waves, allowing them to rise and fall without acting on them.

- **Cognitive defusion:** Create distance from unhelpful thoughts by labeling them as just thoughts, not facts.

- **Values clarification:** Reconnect with personal values to strengthen motivation for recovery.

- **Craving metaphors:** Create personalized metaphors for cravings (e.g., a monster, a storm) to externalize and manage them more effectively.

- **Thought stopping:** Interrupt negative thought patterns by using a physical cue or mental image.

Behavioral Strategies

- **HALT check:** Address Hunger, Anger, Loneliness, or Tiredness, which can trigger cravings.

- **Behavioral activation:** Engage in positive activities that provide natural rewards.

- **Opposite action:** Act opposite to the urge to use substances.

- **Distraction techniques:** Engage in activities that occupy the mind and body.

- **Relaxation exercises:** Practice deep breathing, progressive muscle relaxation, or meditation.

- **Cue exposure:** Gradually expose yourself to triggers in a controlled environment to build resilience.

Emotional Regulation Strategies

- **Emotional awareness:** Identify and label emotions without judgment.

- **Acceptance:** Embrace difficult emotions without trying to change or avoid them.

- **Self-soothing:** Use sensory experiences to calm intense emotions.

- **Radical acceptance:** Accept the reality of cravings without struggling against them.

- **Emotional regulation skills:** Learn and practice techniques to manage intense emotions effectively.

- **Emotion surfing:** Similar to urge surfing, ride out intense emotions without acting on them.

Interpersonal Strategies

- **Build a support network:** Connect with supportive individuals who understand recovery challenges.

- **Assertiveness training:** Learn to express needs and set boundaries effectively.

- **Interpersonal effectiveness:** Improve communication skills to navigate relationships without substances.

- **Seek accountability:** Share struggles with a sponsor or trusted friend.

- **Group therapy participation:** Engage in peer support to learn from others' experiences.

- **Role-playing:** Practice handling difficult situations or conversations in a safe environment.

Lifestyle Strategies

- **Establish routine:** Create a structured daily schedule to reduce triggers and increase stability.

- **Self-care practices:** Prioritize sleep, nutrition, and exercise to support overall well-being.

- **Develop new hobbies:** Explore interests that provide fulfillment and purpose without substances.

- **Mindfulness-based relapse prevention:** Integrate mindfulness practices into daily life to prevent relapse.

- **Committed action:** Set and pursue goals aligned with personal values to create a meaningful life in recovery.

- **Gratitude practice:** Regularly acknowledge and appreciate positive aspects of life in recovery.

- **Volunteering:** Engage in community service to foster a sense of purpose and connection.

Sustained recovery depends on having a plan and putting it into action. Each time you apply these strategies, you build strength and resilience. The ability to manage cravings and regulate emotions improves with practice.

No single approach works for everyone. The key is to integrate different strategies and find what fits your needs. Over time, cravings lose their power and emotional balance becomes easier to maintain.

Recovery means more than abstaining from substances. It is about creating a stable and fulfilling life.

CHAPTER EIGHT

Understanding And Managing Cravings

Cravings demand attention, hijack thoughts, and make relief seem just one drink away. They don't care about goals or progress. And when they hit, they hit hard.

But cravings don't have to win. Even when they feel overwhelming, there are ways to loosen their grip. Managing them doesn't mean they disappear overnight, but each time they're handled differently, they lose a little power.

What Triggers a Craving?

Sometimes, the trigger is obvious—standing in line at a convenience store, staring at a cooler filled with beer, or feeling drained after a long shift. Other times, it's more subtle. A sudden restlessness, a weight in the chest, or an unsettled stomach can signal an urge before the mind catches up.

Not all triggers make sense in the moment. Cravings don't just come from thoughts; they stem from emotional and physical patterns shaped over time. Recognizing this can make them easier to approach with curiosity instead of frustration.

How to Ride Out a Craving

Cravings rise, peak, and fade. They don't stay at full intensity forever, even if it feels that way. Trying to fight them head-on often strengthens them. But riding them out—letting them build and break—takes away some of their control.

Urge surfing helps. A craving is like a wave. Instead of thrashing against it, let it swell and trust that it will recede. It might not feel easy, but it will pass.

Delay, Distract, Decide is another approach. When an urge crashes in, step back. Wait before responding. Shift focus—step outside, listen to music, text someone. Once the moment dulls, decide what happens next. Cravings push for quick action, but adding space weakens their urgency.

Then there's **reframing the thought**. Instead of "I need a drink," shift to "I want a drink, but I don't have to act on this feeling." The craving doesn't disappear, but it becomes one thought among many, not an order to follow.

When the Reason Isn't Clear

Some cravings make sense. Others come without warning. That's because urges aren't just about thoughts—they're also about body responses. Tension in the chest, a jittery sensation, or unease can surface before the mind understands why.

Managing cravings isn't just about reasoning through them. Sometimes, there's nothing to reason with. Learning to sit with discomfort—even when it doesn't make sense—helps. Whether the urge has a clear trigger or not, the same tools apply: ride it out, delay the response, and remember that it will pass.

Breaking the Chain Reaction

Cravings follow a pattern. A situation sparks a feeling, which leads to a thought, which fuels an urge. Maybe it starts with exhaustion, leading to "Drinking would fix this." That thought feeds frustration or anxiety, making alcohol seem inevitable.

But it isn't. That chain can be broken. Changing just one part—like shifting "I need a drink" to "I need something to help, but it doesn't have to be alcohol"—leads to a different outcome. The feeling might not disappear immediately, but it stops driving the same automatic response.

Tools for Handling Urges

- **Cognitive Restructuring:** Cravings come with thoughts that feel like truth. Challenge them. Ask, "Is this my only option? What else might help?"

- **Mindfulness and Acceptance:** Some cravings can't be talked away. Acknowledge them without letting them dictate what happens next.

- **Healthy Coping Strategies:** Exercise, journaling, deep breathing, music, reaching out to someone—different things work for different people. Finding what helps takes trial and error.

Creating a Life That Supports Change

A strong foundation weakens cravings. Taking care of physical health—rest, nutrition, movement—makes a difference. Having supportive people around helps. Focusing on meaningful goals shifts attention away from cravings.

Cravings are frustrating. They can feel relentless. But they aren't permanent or unbeatable. Each time a craving is faced and not followed, it loses power.

The next chapter explores Shadowframe images—a tool to externalize cravings and urges, giving them form outside the mind. By making them something visible and separate, it becomes easier to recognize their influence and take back control.

CHAPTER NINE

The Shadowframe Method™

A VISUAL INTERVENTION STRATEGY FOR ADDICTION URGES

A friend of mine once told me a story. When she was a child, she used to look down the road and see an old tree stump that she thought looked like a bear. She was terrified of it. One day she decided that she was going to stare down that bear. She stared it down until it became nothing but the tree stump it really was. From that point on, she learned that we must "stare down our monsters." This is what I created the Shadowframe Method to do. I later realized that it is useful for so much more.

The Shadowframe Method is a unique and deeply personal approach to breaking the cycle of addiction urges. By externalizing the struggle, individuals can gain clarity, interrupt harmful patterns, and reclaim control. Whether created by hand or through guided assistance from ChatGPT, the Shadowframe Image serves as a constant, powerful reminder that the urge is separate—and that we have the strength to overcome it. The Shadowframe Method is based upon an ACT strategy of personifying emotions or thoughts. With the help of AI, this method is now trained into ChatGPT for anyone to use as an urge-management tool in their journey toward self-mastery and resilience.

How Shadowframe Images Fit Into Recovery

Shadowframe Images are a new and deeply personal tool for helping someone visualize their recovery journey. They aren't a rigid method or an established practice; instead, they offer a creative and flexible approach to exploring emotions, challenges, and growth. Whether they reflect struggles, triumphs, or lessons learned, these images allow for a unique way of connecting with the recovery process. Alex, a theoretical character readers will come to know in this book, provides a way to explore how these images might look and feel. Through Alex's hypothetical experiences, it's possible to imagine how Shadowframe Images could fit into someone's recovery journey.

Alex's First Shadowframe: Facing the Urge

In the early days of recovery, Alex struggled with cravings that felt overwhelming. The feelings seemed to come out of nowhere, sudden and strong, making Alex question their ability to stay on track. To make sense of it all, Alex might create a Shadowframe Image to reflect what those cravings felt like—a dense, shadowy forest with glowing eyes peering out from between the trees. This image would represent the cravings as something external, something Alex could see and confront instead of being consumed by them. By capturing this experience in visual form, Alex might feel a sense of control, a moment to pause and reflect: "This is what I'm facing, but it doesn't define me. I can step away from this." The act of creating the image itself could be grounding, offering a way to process the intensity of those early days.

Shifting Perspectives: Seeing Growth

As Alex moved further into recovery, the cravings became less frequent, and a new sense of clarity began to emerge. Recovery started to feel less like a battle and more like an opportunity to rebuild. In this phase, Alex's Shadowframe Images might shift to reflect growth and progress. Imagine Alex creating an image of a strong tree, its roots deep in the soil and its branches stretching toward the sky. The trunk might bear scars—reminders of the struggles Alex had faced—but the leaves would be vibrant and full of life. Among the branches, Alex could include small symbols of the things recovery had brought back into their life: a sunburst for mornings filled with hope, a tiny book for learning new things, or a small figure representing a mended relationship. This kind of Shadowframe might serve as a reminder of the strength Alex was building and the good things recovery was making possible. It would be a visual affirmation, something Alex could look at during moments of doubt to remember how far they'd come.

Reflecting on the Past: Learning Through Shadows

Recovery isn't only about looking forward—it's also about acknowledging the past. For Alex, this might mean creating a Shadowframe that reflects the impact of addiction. One image could be a cracked mirror on a table, surrounded by scattered pieces of glass. In the reflection, Alex might include symbols of what addiction had taken—a shadowed chair for a lost relationship, a dark cloud for the weight of anxiety, or an empty space for missed opportunities. But the image wouldn't end there. In one corner of the reflection, Alex might include a flickering candle, its flame small but steady. This would symbolize the hope and resilience that carried Alex through those difficult times, a reminder that even in the darkest moments, there was light. This kind of Shadowframe isn't about guilt or shame. Instead, it's about honoring the truth of the journey—recognizing the lessons of the past while continuing to move forward.

Celebrating Recovery: Embracing the Light

As recovery deepened, Shadowframe Images could become a way for Alex to celebrate the joys of sobriety. One of Alex's later images might show a peaceful forest path, sunlight streaming through the trees. Along the path could be symbols of the positive changes in Alex's life: a blooming flower for renewed health, a guitar for rediscovered passions, or a group of smiling figures representing strengthened friendships. This type of image would be a reminder of why recovery matters—not just to escape the struggles of addiction, but to embrace the beauty of life on the other side. It would represent not only what Alex had achieved but also the future they were building.

The Many Faces of Shadowframes

Shadowframe Images are as flexible and dynamic as the recovery journey itself. For Alex, each image might serve a different purpose—one to face the intensity of cravings, another to reflect on growth, and yet another to honor the lessons of the past. As readers encounter Alex later in the book, they'll see this character grappling with their own recovery journey in various prompts and scenarios. Shadowframe Images provide a way to explore that journey visually, offering a creative space to process emotions and experiences. They are not a set formula or a one-size-fits-all solution. Instead, they are an invitation to connect with recovery in a deeply personal way. No matter where someone is on their path, Shadowframe Images are a blank canvas—ready to hold the truths, challenges, and victories of recovery. They grow and change as the person creating them grows and changes, reflecting where they've been and where they're going.

How to Create a Shadowframe Image

A Shadowframe Image is a personal visual representation of your addiction urges, externalizing them in a way that makes their influence tangible. The process of creating one—whether through drawing, painting, or digital design—helps you step outside the immediate intensity of the craving and see it as something separate from yourself. Below is a step-by-step guide to crafting your own Shadowframe Image, whether by hand or with digital tools.

Steps to Creating a Shadowframe Image

1. Personify the Urge

Your addiction urge is not just a feeling—it has a presence.

- *If it were a creature, entity, or force, what would it look like?*

- *Does it take a monstrous form, something grotesque or shadowy?*

- *Is it deceptive, appearing alluring but harboring menace beneath?*

- *How does it interact with you—does it whisper, pull, hover, or lurk?*

What emotions does it bring when it appears—fear, exhaustion, temptation, or desperation?

2. Visualize the Setting

- *Where does this entity exist in your mind's eye? The setting helps establish the emotional tone of the image.*

- *Is it a dark alley, a twisted forest, an empty room, or a chaotic landscape?*

- *Do the surroundings reinforce its hold over you—oppressive, tempting, or overwhelming?*

- *Are there small details that make the place feel personal, like familiar objects distorted by its presence?*

3. Depict Your Role in the Image

- *How do you appear in the scene? Consider your posture, expression, and the way you interact with the entity.*

- *Are you being manipulated, drained, or controlled? Is there fear, sadness, or exhaustion on your face?*

- *Does the entity loom over you, whispering in your ear, pulling at you, or feeding off your hesitation?*

- *Shadowframe images make it easier to recognize that the craving is an external force, not your identity.*

Creating an Artistic Shadowframe Image by Hand

If you're comfortable with drawing or painting, creating your Shadowframe Image by hand allows you to fully engage with the process.

Tips for Artistic Creation:

- *Sketch first – Let the image emerge without judgment. Even rough lines can capture the essence of the urge.*

- *Use colors purposefully – Darker tones may express weight and oppression, while sharp contrasts can evoke conflict.*

- *Focus on emotion over realism – The image doesn't have to be perfect; it just has to feel real to you.*

- *Experiment with abstract representation – If you don't want to depict a literal figure, use shapes, movement, or surreal elements to convey the urge's energy.*

- *If traditional materials feel restrictive, consider using other digital apps that allow for layering and flexibility.*

Creating a Shadowframe Image Online

If drawing by hand isn't an option for you, you can work with ChatGPT to generate a your own personalized Shadowframe Image. To begin, simply type: *"I want to create a Shadowframe Image."* This will begin a guided process where ChatGPT asks reflective questions to refine your concept, translating your responses into a visual representation.

Using Your Shadowframe Image as a Recovery Tool

Once your image is complete, it becomes more than art—it's a tool for confronting urges with clarity.

Keep it visible – Set it as a desktop background, phone wallpaper, or print it out to place somewhere you'll see it regularly.

Use it in moments of temptation – When cravings strike, take a moment to look at the image. Recognize that this urge is not you—it is separate, an entity that does not define your willpower.

Reflect on its meaning over time — As you progress, your relationship with the image may change. Consider updating it to reflect your growing strength and detachment from the addiction.

In sum, the Shadowframe Method is a unique and deeply personal approach to breaking the cycle of addiction urges. By externalizing the struggle, individuals can gain clarity, interrupt harmful patterns, and reclaim control. Whether created by hand or through guided assistance from AI, the Shadowframe Image serves as a constant, powerful reminder that the urge is separate from us—and that we have the strength to overcome it. The Shadowframe Method is based upon an ACT strategy of personifying emotions or thoughts. With the help of AI, this method is now trained into ChatGPT for anyone to use as an urge-management tool in their journey toward self-mastery and resilience.

CHAPTER TEN

Relapse

THE ENEMY YOU NEVER SEE COMING --- UNTIL YOU DO

Let's Talk About Relapse

When you quit drinking and commit to lifelong sobriety, you mean it. You mean it with every ounce of resolve in your body. But here's the truth—if you don't fully understand relapse, you're walking into battle blind. That empty glass clinking down on the table in front of you? You never saw it coming.

Nobody plans for relapse. You plan for recovery. You pour everything into staying sober. But the reality is, if you are serious—truly serious—about sobriety, then you have to be just as relentless in learning about relapse as you are in swearing off that last drink. In some ways, understanding relapse is more important than simply making the decision to quit.

And let's be clear: this isn't just about skimming through a few warnings or memorizing a list of risk factors. This section isn't here to teach you about relapse—it's here to make sure you learn it. To make sure you know it. To make sure it becomes second nature. Because too many relapses look like they came out of nowhere—until you look back, armed with the right knowledge, and realize all the warning signs were flashing the whole time.

If you're reading this, you are—or will be—a Recovery Ally. Maybe you're a therapist, a doctor, a recovery group leader. Maybe you're a friend, a spouse, a partner. Maybe you're someone fighting for your own survival. Whatever role you play, you need to know what relapse looks like. You need to recognize it before it happens. And when it does? You need to know exactly how to act.

So get ready. This is serious. For some, what you learn here will be the difference between life and death.

Relapse: The Invisible Descent Before the First Drink

Relapse isn't what most people think it is. It's not just that moment when someone picks up a drink. It doesn't happen in an instant, and it's not a single bad decision made in a flash of weakness. That's not how it works. It starts way before that. Long before alcohol is even in the picture. It begins in the mind, in the emotions, in the habits that shift ever so slightly. It sneaks in quietly, through stress, through exhaustion, through isolation, through the dangerous belief that maybe things aren't so bad.

For many people, relapse is a slow, downward pull. It doesn't just happen. It builds. It gains momentum in ways that don't seem obvious at first. It chips away at the foundation little by little. A Recovery Ally, whether that's a friend, a spouse, a therapist, a sponsor, or even someone acting as their own ally, has to be able to recognize it before it gains strength. The earlier it's caught, the easier it is to stop. But if it goes unnoticed? If it's allowed to progress unchecked? That's when the moment happens—the drink in hand, the buzz in the body, the stunned realization that the line has been crossed. And once that line is crossed, it's too late to stop what's already in motion. It starts in the mind before it ever reaches the hands.

It starts with small justifications, quiet conversations with yourself. One drink won't hurt. Maybe this whole sobriety thing was an overreaction. Maybe drinking wasn't the real problem. Maybe this time will be different. The mind rehearses the possibility long before the body acts on it. And once the mind starts negotiating, the battle is already halfway lost.

Relapse doesn't hit like a lightning strike. It doesn't announce itself. It creeps in. It hides behind frustration, behind complacency, behind the idea that things are finally under control. It disguises itself as overconfidence. It slips in through old habits—staying up too late, skipping meetings, ignoring emotions. It starts with a feeling of disconnect, a sense of unease, a slow drift away from the things that were keeping sobriety strong.

But relapse isn't inevitable. It can be stopped before it happens—if you know what to look for. That's why this matters. That's why this is being hammered into place. Because too many people look back at relapse and think, I should have seen that coming. Too many Recovery Allies, whether supporting a loved one or fighting their own battle, recognize the warning signs only in hindsight. And by then, it's too late.

That's why this is serious. That's why this has to be understood, not just skimmed over. This is the difference between staying sober and slipping back. This is the difference between recognizing the first crack in the foundation and waiting until the whole thing collapses. If you don't see a relapse forming, you can't stop it. But if you do—if you know exactly how it begins, how it grows, how it pulls someone back in—you can break the pattern before it ever reaches the point of no return.

This is what every Recovery Ally needs to know. Whether you're supporting someone you love or standing guard over your own sobriety, this is the knowledge that matters. This is what makes the difference. This is what will be hammered home, again and again, until it's not just something you've read—it's something you understand.

Stage One: Emotional Relapse – The Spark

The first stage of relapse doesn't even feel like relapse. That's what makes it so dangerous. Emotional relapse isn't about wanting to drink; it's about not taking care of yourself in the ways that keep you strong in recovery. You start getting overwhelmed, but instead of dealing with it, you push through, telling yourself you're fine. Except you're not.

Maybe you start skipping meals, sleeping poorly, or snapping at people for no reason. You stop opening up about how you're feeling, either because you think you shouldn't complain or because you don't want to deal with it. Little by little, the things that kept you steady—your routines, your support system, your self-awareness—start to slip away. You don't even notice at first. But that's the problem.

Then the exhaustion kicks in. The stress piles up. You're emotionally drained, mentally foggy, and physically wiped. You're running on fumes, and when that happens, your brain starts looking for the quickest way to feel better. This is where relapse starts, even though drinking isn't on your mind yet. The setup is in place. Now, all it takes is a little push.

Life can be busy. Life can be stressful. Life can have many roadblocks that threaten to take us off course. We're riding along through our daily routine. Emotions like anxiety and overwhelm creep in. Stress wears us down. That stress... that anxiety... the physical exhaustion... You know what you're feeling, but you don't recognize that these were also the patterns that addiction hardwired into your brain. Emotional relapse sets up a resonance that builds into a tsunami. When the brain FEELS those old emotional patterns, the old wiring becomes activated. It's the addictive brain that has come back into action. If we're not watching, the results of alcohol addiction turn the brain into a game of chutes and ladders. If we don't stay alert for the problem signs, then when the signs of emotional relapse happen, down a chute we go. The Recovery Ally must be vigilant at all times. Where recovery is concerned, a rock-solid understanding of the insidious stages of relapse can mean the difference between finding the ladders or tumbling down the chutes.

Emotional relapse doesn't always look the same for everyone. It doesn't have a single script that plays out in the exact same way each time. Some signs may be obvious, others may be subtle, and some may not show up at all. That's why it's important to understand that relapse isn't defined by a checklist—it's defined by a shift. A change. A movement away from stability and toward something riskier. It may be isolation creeping in, or it may be the opposite—a frantic need to stay busy to avoid facing emotions. It could be exhaustion, trouble sleeping, or suddenly needing more sleep than usual. It may be irritability, frustration, a short fuse, or a numb, detached feeling. It may be cravings, or it may just be thinking more about the past—romanticizing old drinking days, questioning whether things were really as bad as they seemed.

Not all signs will be there, and not all will look the same. Some people will notice defensiveness when asked about their recovery. Others may not experience defensiveness at all but may find themselves pulling away from accountability, avoiding conversations, or subtly rewriting their own history in their mind. Dishonesty doesn't always mean lying outright. Sometimes, it's about avoiding the truth, even from yourself. It's about justifying small compromises, convincing yourself that maybe your boundaries don't need to be so firm, that maybe you've outgrown the need for structure, that maybe you were too extreme in your approach.

That's why this isn't a checklist—it's a collection of possibilities. The important thing isn't whether every single sign applies. The important thing is recognizing when something is shifting. Recognizing when patterns start changing, when thoughts start bending in directions that make drinking seem like less of a risk than it really is. This is about knowing yourself, knowing your own patterns, and watching for the moments where things feel off—even if you can't quite put your finger on why.

Recognizing and Responding to the Process of Emotional Relapse

So, something clicked. You recognize yourself in these words. Maybe you're realizing you've been moving through emotional relapse for a while. Maybe you're feeling trapped in a life situation that you can't immediately change—marital stress, financial struggles, a job that demands more than you can give. Maybe you feel powerless.

Stop. Take a breath. You are not powerless. Emotional relapse is a process, but at any point in that process, you can take action to disrupt it before it leads you further down.

Start by grounding yourself in the present. You don't have to fix everything today. Just focus on now. Breathe—deep and slow. Hold it. Exhale. Repeat until your heart rate settles. Say it out loud: "I am struggling, but I am still in control of my choices." Engage your senses. Look around and name five things you see, four things you can touch, three things you hear, two things you smell, and one thing you taste. This moment is real. Stay in it.

Do something small to take care of yourself. When life feels too big, start tiny. Eat something nourishing. Drink a glass of water. Step outside for five minutes. Stretch. Play a song that makes you feel calmer or stronger. Just one thing—because one thing leads to another.

Talk to someone. You don't have to do this alone. Reach out. Call or text a friend, a sponsor or Ally, or someone who understands. If speaking feels too hard, send a message: "I'm struggling." And if no one is immediately available, write it down. Get those thoughts out of your head and onto paper.

Remind yourself why you chose recovery. Stress is real. Struggles are real. But drinking won't fix them. Say it aloud: "I didn't get sober just to go back." "I know what happens when I drink, and it doesn't make anything better." "I deserve a life that is bigger than addiction."

Shift your environment. If you feel stuck, move. Step outside. Change rooms. Reorganize your space. Take a shower. Your surroundings shape your mindset—adjust them to support you.

You don't have to solve everything right now, but you do need to take care of yourself right now. Recovery isn't about perfection; it's about learning to live within life's imperfections without turning to alcohol. Even in the hardest moments, you have power. The fact that you're here, recognizing what's happening, wanting to change course—that's proof of it.

Stage 2: Mental Relapse – The Smoke

Once emotional relapse has you worn down, your thoughts start shifting. This is the mental relapse stage—the battle inside your head between wanting to stay sober and the growing temptation to drink.

At first, it's just little thoughts. Random memories of drinking pop up, and instead of shutting them down, you entertain them. You start remembering the good times, conveniently forgetting the black-outs, the shame, the wreckage. Then the bargaining starts: Maybe I wasn't really that bad. Maybe I could handle it now. Just one drink wouldn't hurt.

This is when you start testing yourself. You scroll through old drinking pictures. You drive past the bar just to "see" what's going on. You tell yourself you're just curious, that it's harmless. But deep down, you know it's not. These are warning signs, and if you don't put the brakes on now, you're heading straight for a relapse.

The tricky part is that mental relapse doesn't feel like a crisis—it feels like an option. And that's the danger. The moment drinking starts feeling like an option, you're already in trouble.

Then comes the whisper—memories of drinking that don't seem so bad. You catch yourself thinking, Maybe I wasn't that out of control. Or, Other people drink, why can't I just have one? You don't realize it at first, but you're entertaining the idea of drinking more and more. Maybe you even find yourself casually scrolling through old photos, passing by places where you used to drink, or reconnecting with old friends who still do.

Mental relapse doesn't announce itself with flashing lights and alarms. It slips in through the back door, disguising itself as harmless thoughts, fleeting memories, or little justifications that seem innocent at first. But if you don't catch it early, it picks up momentum, pushing you closer and closer to that moment where saying "no" feels impossible.

For some, mental relapse shows up as nostalgia. You start reminiscing, but only about the "good" times—the laughs, the parties, the relief, the escape. The blackouts, the shame, the consequences? Suddenly, those memories fade into the background. Your mind starts twisting the truth, convincing you that maybe drinking wasn't as bad as you thought. Maybe you used to have fun when you drank. Maybe you overreacted. Maybe you were never really that bad.

For others, it arrives as bargaining. The internal negotiations begin. You start looking for loopholes, trying to convince yourself that drinking could somehow fit into your life again—just in a controlled way. Maybe just on weekends. Maybe just socially. Maybe just something "light." One drink wouldn't hurt. You can handle it now. You've been sober for a while, so you deserve a break. Recovery stops feeling like a commitment to yourself and starts feeling like a rulebook full of technicalities.

Then there are those who experience mental relapse as a slow, creeping desire. The thoughts start small but build. You romanticize drinking, picturing that first sip like a long-lost lover. You imagine the taste, the feeling, the comfort—without the wreckage that follows. It's like watching a highlight reel, where all the worst parts of drinking have been edited out. Drinking used to make you feel so relaxed. Maybe you just want to shut your brain off for a while.

Maybe you don't feel the nostalgia or the bargaining, but instead, you start flirting with the idea of drinking without fully realizing it. Without planning to, you start seeking out triggers. You drive by the old bar. You scroll through old drinking photos. You reconnect with friends who still drink. You tell yourself it's harmless, that you're just curious, that you're just testing yourself. I'll just stop by and say hi. I won't drink. I can be around it. I have self-control now. But deep down, you know what you're doing.

For some, it's not memories or curiosity—it's avoidance. You stop engaging with recovery, not because you plan to drink, but because you're tired of thinking about it. You tell yourself you don't need to go to that meeting, that you're fine skipping check-ins. Maybe you don't want to admit that the thoughts are creeping in, so you isolate instead. You stop answering texts from sober friends. You skip meetings. You don't want to hear them say what you already know—you're playing with fire. Maybe you tell yourself you're just busy. Maybe you convince yourself you don't need to talk about it. No one needs to know what you're thinking. You can handle this on your own. But isolation is the perfect breeding ground for relapse. The further you drift from your support system, the easier it becomes to convince yourself that drinking is an option.

Mental relapse is a mind game, and if you don't shut it down early, it gets stronger. It wears you down, little by little, until the thought of drinking doesn't seem like a choice anymore—it feels inevitable.

But here's the thing: it's not. The moment you recognize these warning signs, you still have the power to stop them. Talk to someone. Say it out loud. Call it what it is. Mental relapse thrives in secrecy—but once you drag it into the light, its grip on you weakens.

Relapse doesn't hit like an earthquake. It starts with a whisper. The sooner you catch it, the easier it is to silence.

Maybe your mental relapse doesn't look like anything that's been described so far. Maybe it's subtle in a way that only you would notice—a certain restlessness, a discontent creeping in. Maybe it's boredom, feeling like sobriety has lost its spark. Maybe it's a resentment you can't shake. Maybe it's feeling like you're doing all this work and wondering, what's the point? Maybe your mental relapse doesn't look like anything that's been described so far. Maybe it's subtle in a way that only you would notice—a certain restlessness, a discontent creeping in. Maybe it's boredom, feeling like sobriety has lost its spark. Maybe it's a resentment you can't shake. Maybe it's feeling like you're doing all this work and wondering, what's the point?

Mental relapse is different for everyone, but the pattern is the same. It's a slow detachment from recovery, a slow inching toward alcohol before you even realize what's happening. The form it takes doesn't matter as much as the fact that it's happening. The moment you recognize it, the moment you see the shift—that's when you have to act.

What to Do When Mental Relapse Happens

If you're reading this and realizing that you're already deep in mental relapse, take a step back. This doesn't have to go any further. You still have choices, and what you do next matters.

Remind yourself why you chose sobriety in the first place. If you've worked through tools in a recovery group, with a therapist, or on your own, pull them out now and revisit them. This isn't about proving anything to yourself—it's about remembering what's real.

Depending on your mindset, pulling yourself out of this spiral alone might not be realistic. That's not failure. It's just where you are right now. Reach out for the help you need. If this is your first time reading this book, you may not have had the chance to create an action plan for moments like this. But maybe you made one in rehab, with a therapist, or with your recovery group. If you did, follow it.

If you don't have a plan, that doesn't mean you're out of options. You once had strong reasons for choosing recovery. Find them. Go back to what convinced you to stop drinking in the first place. If you can't access those reasons right now, reach out to someone who can remind you—someone who has supported you before or someone with the skills to help you regain stability.

If you've had this book for a while, remember that The Alcohol Recovery Ally provides tools for moments like this. If you've created an action plan, use it. Maybe you wrote down your reasons for staying sober or memorized what to do in a crisis. Now is the time to act on that preparation.

If this is your first time reading this, and you don't have a plan, that's okay. You don't need a perfect plan to make the right choice. The most important thing right now is to reach out. You don't have to figure this out alone. Call someone. Find a meeting. Talk to a friend. Seek out a therapist or a support group. Say the words: "I am struggling. I need help."

Mental relapse thrives in secrecy. The longer you sit in it, the stronger it gets. Say it out loud. Break the silence. Acknowledge what's happening so you can stop it in its tracks. The deeper into mental relapse you go, the harder it is to pull yourself back—but no stage is too late.

This isn't the moment—it's a moment. A turning point, just like emotional relapse was, just like any slip or relapse will be if that happens. You don't have to make every right decision for the rest of your life. You just have to make the right decision right now. There's still time. You're not out of options. Take the next step, whatever that looks like for you.

Stage 3: The Physical Relapse – The Fire

After a relapse occurs, your mind might be running in a hundred different directions. Regret, shame, frustration, self-doubt. Maybe you're still trying to make sense of it, telling yourself it was just a bad night, a rough week, a slip that doesn't really mean anything. Or maybe you're on the other end, feeling like this relapse proves every worst fear you had about yourself, that you can't do this, that you never really could.

Here's the truth: no matter how far you think you've fallen, you are not stuck there. Relapse doesn't erase all the progress you've made. It doesn't mean you have to stay in the spiral. It's a moment in time, and like every moment before it, you have a choice about what happens next.

The hardest part about relapse isn't the drinking itself—it's what happens after. It's the voice in your head that says, "You already messed up. Might as well keep going." That's the thought that turns a slip into a full relapse. That's the thought that keeps you in the cycle. And it's a lie. You don't have to keep going. You don't have to prove anything to anyone, including yourself. The only thing you have to do is stop and take the next right step.

Maybe your body is feeling it—exhaustion, nausea, dehydration, that hollowed-out feeling that reminds you why you quit in the first place. Maybe your mind won't shut up, running through every reason you failed or every excuse for why this was inevitable. Maybe your emotions are tangled—shame, relief, regret, denial, all fighting for space in your chest. Or maybe you feel nothing at all, just numbness, because it's easier than dealing with the reality of where you are. Whatever you're feeling, however your body is reacting, it's real. And it's temporary. What happens next determines how long you sit in this place.

Hiding it won't help. Keeping it a secret won't undo it. If anything, that will only make it worse. Secrecy feeds shame, and shame fuels relapse. If you don't want this to spiral further, the first step is telling the truth—at least to yourself. Say it out loud. "I drank." No explanations. No justifications. Just the truth. And then decide what happens next.

Maybe you've been in this place before, and you already know what helps. Maybe you had a plan for this moment, one you set up when you were still sober and thinking clearly. If you do, follow it. If you don't, you can still make one now. You don't need to have all the answers—you just need to take the next right step. Reach out. Call someone. Go to a meeting. Get back to what was working for you before. Or, if nothing was working before, figure out what needs to change.

If the relapse has lasted longer than a slip, you might be feeling the full weight of it—physically, emotionally, mentally, even socially or legally. Maybe you lost trust with people who believed in you. Maybe you're facing consequences that feel too big to handle. Maybe your own mind is the worst place to be right now, because it won't let you forget what happened. You don't have to have all the answers today. You just have to decide that this isn't where your story ends.

You're not starting over. You're continuing. You still have every lesson, every piece of knowledge, every bit of growth that came from your time in sobriety. The relapse, too, holds many lessons that can strengthen your resolve. You still have a choice. And in that decisive moment of reflection after the relapse, that choice is a fork in the road. One path continues down the road of addiction, the other leads toward recovery. You already know which one leads you to the life you actually want. You don't have to have it all figured out—just take the next step when you're ready.

CHAPTER ELEVEN

Guilt, Shame, And The Alcohol Trap

UNDERSTANDING WHAT'S REALLY HAPPENING

The Cultural Contradiction of Alcohol and Addiction

Alcohol is everywhere. It's at weddings, birthdays, office parties, and even at the end of a long day as a way to "unwind." Drinking is not just accepted—it's often expected.

But there's a catch-22: society encourages drinking, yet condemns addiction. People drink to fit in, celebrate, or cope, but if their drinking crosses an invisible line, they are often met with judgment and shame.

Nobody starts drinking with the mindset of *"This will take over my life."* Yet, for some, alcohol gradually becomes something they need rather than something they choose. By the time problems arise, the same culture that embraced drinking now labels the person as weak or morally flawed. This contradiction creates a breeding ground for guilt and shame, making it even harder to break free.

Guilt vs. Shame: What's the Difference?

To work through these emotions, it's important to understand them:

Guilt: *"I did something wrong."* (Focuses on actions)

Shame: *"There's something wrong with me."* (Focuses on identity)

Example: Emily used to drink socially, but over time, she started drinking alone. She forgot important commitments and lost a close friendship. She feels **guilty** for breaking promises, but when she starts believing, *I'm a horrible person. I ruin everything, ...* That's **shame. It's** a much deeper wound.

Guilt can be constructive—it can push people to make amends and change. But shame is crippling—it makes people believe they are beyond help. And in the case of alcohol addiction, shame often fuels the very behavior a person is trying to escape.

How To Let Go Of The Shame: The Facts

Understand How Alcohol Hijacks the Mind, Body, and Emotions

Alcohol doesn't just affect behavior—it rewires the brain and body, sometimes leading to thoughts, actions, or feelings that feel completely out of character. Many people look back on things they did while drinking and think, *That wasn't me. Why did I act that way?*

Here's why:

The Brain and Decision-Making

Alcohol slows down the prefrontal cortex, the part of the brain responsible for judgment, impulse control, and rational thinking. This means:

Decisions that seem reckless or embarrassing in hindsight made sense at the time.

People say or do things they never would while sober.

It's harder to recognize when things are getting out of control.

Example: Jake always prided himself on being responsible. But after drinking too much one night, he drove home, convinced he was "fine." The next day, he was horrified. His brain had genuinely believed the choice was safe—because alcohol impaired his ability to assess risk.

The Body and Dependence

Alcohol affects neurotransmitters like dopamine and GABA, which regulate mood, stress, and relaxation. Over time:

The brain relies on alcohol to produce pleasure and calmness.

The body craves alcohol just to feel normal.

Without alcohol, withdrawal symptoms like anxiety, agitation, and depression set in.

Example: Lisa didn't start drinking to escape life—she started because it helped her socialize. But after months of drinking daily, she noticed she felt awful without it. Her body had become dependent, and stopping wasn't just a choice—it felt impossible.

Emotions and Self-Perception

Alcohol changes how people process emotions, making it harder to:
Recognize emotional triggers before they spiral.
Separate real thoughts from alcohol-fueled negativity.
Feel confident or hopeful without alcohol.

Example: David felt lonely after a breakup. When drinking, those feelings intensified, and he convinced himself nobody cared about him. In reality, his mind was under the influence of alcohol's depressive effects—exaggerating his pain and self-doubt.

These changes don't happen overnight. By the time someone realizes alcohol is shaping their thoughts, feelings, and behaviors, the cycle is already in motion.

How Shame and Guilt Keep the Cycle Going

Because alcohol changes the brain and body, many behaviors aren't entirely within a person's control. But without this understanding, guilt and shame take over—leading to avoidance, defensiveness, and self-medicating.

Common Responses to Guilt and Shame:

Avoiding the truth (If I don't think about it, it's not real).
Minimizing the problem (*I'm not that bad*).
Blaming others (If my job wasn't so stressful, I wouldn't drink).
Hiding struggles (I can't let people know).
Drinking more to escape the emotions—which only makes them
　　worse.

　　Example: After a relapse, Sarah thought, *I've ruined every-thing. I might as well give up.* Her shame told her she was beyond saving. In reality, her relapse was a result of an emotional trigger and brain chemistry—not a moral failing.

　　Breaking the shame cycle requires a different perspective. Instead of seeing addiction as a personal weakness, it helps to see it as a condition influenced by brain chemistry, emotional responses, and societal contradictions.

Change The Script

You didn't set out to struggle with alcohol—you were in an environment where drinking was normal. The fact that you want to change says more about your strength than your past choices.
Reframe your story: Instead of I failed, try: "I am learning to navi-gate the culture that made alcohol feel like the answer."
Practice self-compassion. If you wouldn't shame a friend for strug-gling, why do it to yourself? Talk to yourself like a friend: When

self-criticism creeps in, ask, What would I say to someone I love in this situation?

Understanding how alcohol affects the brain and emotions can help separate who you are from what alcohol has done. When negative thoughts come up, ask, Is this me, or is this the effect of alcohol withdrawal, stress, or old habits?

Shame thrives in isolation. Opening up to a therapist, support group, or trusted friend weakens its hold. If speaking feels too hard, start by writing down your thoughts as if you were comforting someone else.

Take small steps toward change.

Shame says, You'll never change.

Reality says, Progress happens one step at a time.

Try tracking small wins: Even one sober day or one honest conversation is a victory worth recognizing.

Alcohol addiction doesn't happen in a vacuum. It happens in a culture where drinking is seen as normal, until it isn't. Addiction happens in a brain and body that slowly adapt to alcohol without asking permission. And it happens in a person who, at their core, never intended to lose control. Guilt and shame are not proof of failure. Instead, they are signs that you care, that you want better for your life, and that you are capable of change. You are not your past, your worst moments, or your struggles. If you are a person in recovery, you are reclaiming your mind, body, and future — one step at a time. That's something to be proud of.

Chapter Twelve

Managing Anxiety

Anxiety is more than stress. It is the body and mind reacting to uncertainty, fear, or perceived danger. The heart races, the stomach knots, and thoughts loop without an exit. It can feel like a survival instinct stuck in overdrive. Some people feel it in waves. Others carry it daily. It can be triggered by major life changes, social situations, or even small, everyday stressors.

For those in recovery, anxiety can feel relentless. Sobriety removes the escape that substances once provided. Emotions that were numbed for years come rushing back, sometimes all at once. Social situations feel unfamiliar. The body and mind are learning how to function without artificial relief. The world moves fast, and the brain struggles to keep up. Anxiety thrives in unpredictability, and early recovery is full of unknowns.

But anxiety is not only about sobriety. It is also the lingering effect of alcohol itself. Drinking disrupts brain chemistry, reducing the body's ability to regulate stress naturally. Over time, the brain adapts to alcohol's presence, depending on it for balance. When drinking stops, that balance is thrown off. The nervous system rebounds, often causing a surge of anxiety that can persist for months. This is not weakness. It is biology. For some, it is a difficult adjustment, but understanding what is happening makes a difference.

Emotions play a powerful role in this process. Alcohol may have once been a way to dull stress or escape painful feelings, but without it, emotions feel bigger, sharper, and harder to control. Frustration can turn into anger. Sadness can feel unbearable. Anxiety can make everything seem overwhelming. But emotions are not the enemy. They are part of healing. Learning to sit with them instead of avoiding them is what makes long-term stability possible, not just in sobriety but in life.

Sleep can make this process even harder. Many people in recovery experience insomnia, even when they are exhausted. The brain is recalibrating, and that can throw sleep completely off balance. Restless nights make anxiety worse, turning exhaustion into frustration. When sleep is disrupted, emotional regulation becomes even more difficult. It may seem like another impossible hurdle, but this will not last forever. Over time, sleep improves, and there are ways to support that process.

Smoking can add another layer of difficulty. Many people assume nicotine helps with stress, but research suggests it does the opposite. Nicotine and alcohol affect some of the same pathways in the brain, reinforcing dependence and making it harder for the body to regain stability. Some studies suggest that smoking during recovery slows the brain's ability to heal from alcohol use. It can also worsen sleep problems, keeping the nervous system on edge and interfering with deep, restorative rest. While quitting everything at once is not the right choice for everyone, being aware of these connections is important. The more the body and brain can heal, the more stable recovery becomes.

For those trying to understand this journey, whether personally or as a supporter, it is important to recognize that recovery is not just about quitting drinking. It is about retraining the brain to handle life in a way that feels sustainable. That process takes time, but the body and mind are built to adapt. Anxiety may feel permanent, but it is not. Every effort in recovery rewires the brain and strengthens emotional resilience. This is not about pushing through with willpower. It is about learning how to live fully. Progress is not always obvious, but healing is happening, even when it does not feel that way yet.

Building Stability When Everything Feels Uncertain

Anxiety thrives in uncertainty. The brain looks for danger, scanning for threats, even when none exist. Stability disrupts this cycle. A sense of control, no matter how small, helps anxiety lose its grip.

One of the simplest ways to create stability is through routines. They do not have to be big or complicated. A morning stretch, a deep breath before work, or a quiet moment before bed can bring relief. Familiar habits tell the brain that things are okay. Even when the world feels chaotic, these rituals create a steady rhythm. Physical movement can help too. A short walk or a few deep breaths shift focus away from anxious thoughts and back into the present.

Connection provides another layer of support. Humans are wired for it. A check-in with a friend, a shared laugh, or a quiet moment with a pet can reset the mind. It does not have to be a deep conversation. Simple interactions remind people they are not alone.

The body plays a role in calming the mind. Anxiety sends signals, but the body can send signals back. Sunlight, fresh air, and movement tell the nervous system that everything is okay. Stepping outside between tasks, cracking open a window, or noticing the way the sky changes can shift emotions. Engaging the senses—listening to music, breathing deeply, stretching, or focusing on a comforting scent—can calm the nervous system. Everyone responds differently. The key is paying attention to what works.

Anxiety and Communication

For many, anxiety can influence how people feel, think, speak, and listen. As a result, conversations may feel more challenging. In these moments, words might not come out as intended. Because of this, the fear of saying the wrong thing can lead to avoidance. Some people withdraw, while others over-explain. In many cases, anxiety can create distance where connection is needed.

Furthermore, this difficulty can become even more pronounced in moments of heightened stress. When anxiety is high, difficult conversations can feel overwhelming. As a result, thoughts may cycle through possible outcomes, making it harder to express what needs to be said. For some, the fear of conflict leads to hesitation. The worry of being judged or dismissed can make it tempting to stay silent. When important feelings go unspoken, tension may build over time.

When anxiety is high, difficult conversations can feel overwhelming. Thoughts may cycle through possible outcomes, making it harder to express what needs to be said. For some, the fear of conflict leads to hesitation. The worry of being judged or dismissed can make it tempting to stay silent. When important feelings go unspoken, tension may build over time.

Naming emotions reduces their power. Instead of thinking, "I feel terrible," breaking it down helps. Saying, "I feel anxious about this meeting," brings clarity. It does not fix the problem, but it makes it feel more manageable. Journaling can help with this. Writing down thoughts before a conversation allows time to process emotions and find the right words.

Anxiety often disguises itself as something else. Frustration can mask fear. Defensiveness can cover up insecurity. Irritability can hide exhaustion. It is easy to react to the surface emotion without questioning what is underneath. Slowing down and asking, "What else am I feeling?" can bring awareness to the real source of distress. That awareness creates space for a different response.

Old emotional patterns can make this even harder. Some people freeze when criticized. Others get defensive without meaning to. Recognizing these patterns is the first step toward change. Awareness makes it possible to choose a different response.

Creating a safe space for communication makes difficult conversations easier. Words come out differently when blame is not part of the equation. Saying, "I feel overwhelmed when..." invites discussion.

Saying, "You never listen," shuts it down. The way something is said matters as much as what is said. When emotions rise, self-soothing, stepping away, or using healthy distractions can prevent a reaction that fuels anxiety.

Rewiring Anxiety's Response

Anxiety tells people to avoid discomfort. That instinct is strong, but it is not always right. Avoidance provides temporary relief, but it makes fear stronger in the long run.

Facing discomfort weakens anxiety's grip. Small, deliberate steps forward help retrain emotional responses. This process, often called the "opposite action" technique, disrupts avoidance patterns. If fear says, "Ignore this," taking even the smallest step forward changes the outcome. A conversation that once seemed impossible becomes easier. A task that once felt overwhelming starts to feel manageable. Each effort builds confidence.

For some, guided breathing or grounding techniques help create enough space to take that first step. Focusing on the breath, squeezing a stress ball, or noticing the feeling of feet on the ground can interrupt anxiety's cycle. The key is finding what works and practicing it when stress levels are low, so it is easier to use in the moment.

This is not an instant fix. Recovery is a process. Managing anxiety is a process. Communication is a process. The goal is not to eliminate anxiety but to learn how to work with it. Small, daily adjustments make a difference. Finding ways to stay present, express needs clearly, and manage emotions without substances creates long-term stability. Every effort, no matter how small, moves things forward.

CHAPTER THIRTEEN

Staying Grounded

Staying Grounded

When challenges come, stability and awareness make it easier to stay in control. Some days feel steady, others shake your confidence, but holding onto the right habits makes all the difference. Staying grounded means knowing where you stand, recognizing what steadies you, and keeping hold of that foundation, especially when emotions threaten to pull you under.

But how do you maintain that stability when life feels unpredictable?

Tracking Your Progress: The Power of Reflection

Journaling is one of the most effective ways to stay centered. Writing things down helps sort through emotions, track patterns, and recognize progress that might otherwise go unnoticed. On days when everything feels uncertain, looking back at past entries provides proof that you have moved forward, even when it does not feel like it.

This does not mean filling pages every day or committing to a structured routine. Even a quick note in your phone or a single sentence on paper can bring clarity. Some people write daily, others only when something feels off. The format does not matter. What matters is taking a moment to check in with yourself.

Some find that using specific prompts makes this process easier. Motivational Interviewing (MI) questions help uncover thoughts and patterns that might not be obvious at first. Even answering one question—What helped me get through today?—can be enough to recognize progress. These prompts are a tool, not a requirement. Try them if they help.

Grounding yourself in reflection strengthens emotional stability. The more aware you are of your patterns, the harder it is to get knocked off course.

But reflection is not limited to private moments on the page. Sometimes, clarity comes through conversation.

Learning from Others: The Value of Community

It is easier to stay steady when surrounded by the right people. Support strengthens stability. The right people provide steadiness when emotions shift, reminding you who you are when doubts creep in.

Recovery happens in connection. Whether through Alcoholics Anonymous, SMART Recovery, therapy, or close personal relationships, having a strong support system offers perspective. The structure is not what matters. It is the connection.

Not everyone has time to attend in-person meetings, but support does not have to be difficult to access. SMART Recovery offers online meetings, and other programs may have virtual options as well. A conversation with one trusted person—whether it is a friend, mentor, or someone who understands—can also make a difference.

Talking through struggles with someone who listens can shift everything. What felt overwhelming suddenly feels manageable. What seemed confusing becomes clear. Some moments bring unexpected clarity, the kind that shifts thinking in a way that lasts. Practicing Freeze-Frame awareness helps create those moments on purpose. Instead of reacting automatically, pausing allows you to regain control and see things differently.

A Recovery Ally can reinforce this kind of stability. Someone who listens without judgment, offers perspective, and encourages reflection can help keep emotions from taking control. The right people make it easier to return to a steady place when everything feels uncertain.

But staying grounded is not just about reacting to difficult moments. A stronger foundation comes from understanding why certain patterns exist in the first place.

Expanding Your Knowledge: Tools for Stability

The more you understand about addiction, emotions, and resilience, the stronger your foundation becomes. Knowledge provides stability by making sense of what is happening beneath the surface.

Books, podcasts, and conversations introduce new ways to navigate challenges. Learning about neuroplasticity reveals how the brain rewires itself, reinforcing new habits. Exploring how stress affects the body makes it easier to recognize tension before it takes over. Understanding boundaries provides the tools to create healthier relationships that support stability rather than disrupt it.

This does not require hours of study or a deep dive into psychology. It can be as simple as listening to a five-minute podcast on the way to work or reading one article that shifts your perspective. Small moments of learning add up.

Recognizing what throws you off balance makes it easier to stay steady. Learning from others, reflecting through journaling, and pausing in the moment all work together to build stability over time.

Growth comes from many places. Reflection, conversation, and learning all reinforce stability, but staying grounded also means having something to look forward to. A meaningful life is not just about avoiding relapse. It is about building something stronger in its place.

Redefining Enjoyment: Finding Stability in New Passions

For years, alcohol might have provided a false sense of steadiness. A way to unwind, to celebrate, to feel in control until it was not anymore.

Letting go of it can feel like losing an anchor, but real stability comes from something stronger.

New experiences create new ways to feel steady. Creative outlets like painting, writing, or music help process emotions. Physical movement like hiking, dancing, or running brings energy and focus. Learning a skill or joining a group creates connection and a sense of progress.

Not everyone has the time or energy to take up a new hobby right away. That is okay. Stability is not about adding more to your plate—it is about making space for what helps. Even ten minutes of something that brings relief can change the course of a day.

At first, these changes might not feel natural. But over time, they become part of who you are. Instead of looking for something to keep you grounded, you become the person who holds steady no matter what comes next.

CHAPTER FOURTEEN

The Emotional Undercurrent Of Recovery

Most people experience emotions like an ocean current. Thoughts and actions drift along the surface while deeper feelings push and pull beneath. Some emotions flow easily without resistance. Others build pressure, shifting thoughts in ways that can be difficult to recognize.

Some people are naturally attuned to their emotions. They can name what they feel and trace it back to its source. Others feel disconnected, unable to put their internal experience into words. In alcohol recovery, learning to recognize these deeper currents is a powerful tool for resilience.

As humans, we are hardwired to experience core emotions: joy, sadness, anger, fear, disgust, and surprise. These emotions are survival mechanisms, deeply ingrained in our biology. But on top of these, we develop secondary emotions such as guilt, shame, anxiety, and frustration, which shape how we interpret the world around us. These secondary emotions can mask what is happening underneath. They can twist our perceptions, making external problems feel larger or disguising internal struggles as something caused by others.

Some emotions are painful, so they get pushed away, often without a person realizing it. But emotions do not disappear. They linger beneath the surface, waiting. When left unprocessed, they build pressure until something such as a disappointment, an argument, or a craving triggers their release. A sudden urge to drink may not come from nowhere. It may be anxiety. It may be loneliness. It may even be joy. Or it may be nothing more than habit. Without awareness, old coping patterns step in. Alcohol once felt like the answer, and in moments of emotional overwhelm, it can feel like the answer again.

Recognizing emotions early can change everything. It creates space between feeling and action, allowing a person to respond instead of react. Learning to pause, reflect, and look deeper than the first reaction can help prevent emotions from taking over.

When emotions feel overwhelming, try this:

- **Stop and take a breath.** Give yourself a moment to reset.

- **Shift from judgment to curiosity.** Ask, "What is really happening here?"

- **Notice physical sensations.** Tight muscles, restlessness, a change in breathing. These can all be clues.

- **Identify triggers.** Did this feeling come from something external? Or is it internal?

- **Find the root.** What sits beneath this emotion? And what sits beneath that?

This process is not always easy. Some emotions carry a weight that feels impossible to hold. But when emotions remain unprocessed, they do not fade. They wait. They build. They rise to the surface when stress, uncertainty, or habit calls them forward.

Developing emotional fluency takes time, but it can make a lasting difference. Increasing awareness of emotions can help:

- Recognize emotional patterns that lead to drinking.

- Lower the risk of impulsive choices.

- Find better ways to cope with difficult feelings.

- Move from reacting to responding with intention.

Building emotional awareness is about learning to sit with uncomfortable emotions without reaching for an escape. It is about staring down the road at that terrifying bear until you see it for what it really is. It is about recognizing patterns before they take control.

What is really underneath an emotion like anger? Is it fear? If it is fear, is it the fear of not being in control? If so, then what is underneath that? Peel back the layers of the onion. The more a person understands what lies beneath the surface of their emotions, the more control they have over their choices.

Try tracking emotional patterns over time. Write them down. Talk about them. Use guided exercises to reflect. Practice self compassion. Emotions are information, not threats.

Developing this level of awareness takes patience, and structure can help. Motivational Interviewing provides a framework for exploring thoughts, uncovering patterns, and shifting behaviors in a meaningful way.

Through this approach, a person can:

- Clarify personal reasons for staying sober.

- Recognize emotional triggers and patterns.

- Reframe challenges to build resilience.

- Understand how past experiences shape current choices.

- Strengthen long term recovery goals through reflection.

The next chapters contain prompts for self discovery and growth. These can be used alone, with a therapist, or with a recovery ally. Each prompt is a tool for exploring emotions more deeply. The more a person engages with them, the clearer their emotional world may become.

And with clarity comes strength.

CHAPTER FIFTEEN

On Motivational Interviewing Prompts

Understanding and managing emotions are crucial components of recovery from Alcohol Use Disorder (AUD). Emotional intelligence—the ability to recognize, understand, and manage our own emotions, as well as empathize with the emotions of others—plays a significant role in this process. Developing emotional intelligence can help individuals in recovery navigate complex feelings, reduce the risk of relapse, and build healthier relationships.

Motivational Interviewing (MI) is an evidence-based counseling approach that enhances motivation and commitment to change by helping individuals explore and resolve ambivalence. In the context of AUD recovery, MI can assist individuals in identifying their personal reasons for change, thereby fostering intrinsic motivation and supporting long-term sobriety.

By integrating emotional intelligence development with Motivational Interviewing techniques, individuals can gain deeper insights into their emotional landscapes and strengthen their commitment to recovery. The following chapters provide a collection of MI prompts designed to facilitate self-reflection, enhance emotional awareness, and support sustained sobriety.

These prompts can be utilized in various ways, including personal journaling, discussions with a therapist or support group, or as part of a structured recovery program. The prompts can be used informally or formally, depending upon the needs of the specific situation at hand. Engaging with these prompts encourages individuals to explore their motivations, identify potential challenges, and develop personalized strategies for maintaining sobriety.

By actively participating in this reflective process, individuals can build a more resilient foundation for their recovery journey, leading to improved emotional well-being and a more fulfilling, sober life.

What follows are examples of motivational interviewing prompts that can be used "as is" or adapted for use by others in supporting roles. The basic categories for exploration include exploring goals and values, encouraging change and action, improving motivation and commitment, reframing thoughts of resistance, uncovering hidden thoughts and emotions, and numerous other topics.

The "you" format can be used directly for self-reflection, including with journaling. It can also be used and adapted by anyone who is working to support an individual in their sobriety journey. Be aware that true Motivational Interviewing (MI) techniques involve layers of questions and validations that go beyond what is possible to replicate here, but these basic questions are a good place to begin. I hope they help.

CHAPTER SIXTEEN

Thinking About Change Prompts

Exploring The Situation

- What brings you here today, and how can I support you in your journey?

- What's the best outcome you could imagine for yourself if you made this change?

- What are some things you've already tried, and how have they worked for you?

- What does a typical day look like for you, and how does this behavior fit into it?

- If nothing changed, how do you think your life might look in 6 months? In a year?

Building on Strengths

- What's something you've accomplished in the past that you're proud of?

- What qualities or skills have helped you overcome challenges before?

- How do you see your strengths helping you in this situation?

- What's a small victory you've had recently, even if it feels unrelated to this?

- Who in your life reminds you of your capabilities and potential?

Weighing The Pros and Cons of Change

- What are the pros and cons of keeping things the way they are?

- What's one thing you'd gain if you decided to change?

- What's one thing you'd lose if you made this change?

- If you were to wake up tomorrow and everything was different, what would have changed?

- What might happen if you don't make any changes?

- What are the benefits of staying the same? What are the drawbacks?

- What's one reason you're considering making this change now?

- How would making this change align with the person you want to be?

Measuring Confidence To Change

- On a scale of 1 to 10, how confident are you in your ability to change? Why?

- What would it take to move you one step closer to a 10?

- If you were 10% more confident, what would you do differently?

- What's the smallest step you could take today toward your goal?

- How will you know when you're ready to make a bigger change?

- What do you think is holding you back from feeling more confident?

Checking The Compass

- How does this behavior fit with the kind of life you want to lead?

- How do you feel about the way this behavior affects your relationships?

- What's something you value deeply, and how does it align with your current behavior?

- How would changing this behavior bring you closer to your personal values?

- What does the future look like if you stay on this path? How does it feel to think about that?

- What's a time in your life when things were better? How does that compare to now?

Gathering Courage To Change

- What's something challenging you've overcome in the past? How did you do it?

- How do you usually approach solving difficult problems in other areas of your life?

- What's one thing you've learned about yourself during this process of change?

- How does it feel to know that even small changes can lead to big results over time?

- What would your life look like if you trusted in your ability to change?

Gathering Supports To Change

- What's something you can do to feel supported during this process?

- Who in your life believes in your ability to succeed?

- What role can your support system play in helping you achieve your goals?

- What resources or tools have helped you in the past that you could use again?

- How can I best support you as you work on these changes?

Exploring Ambivalence To Change

- It sounds like part of you wants to change and part of you isn't sure. Can we talk about that?

- What are some reasons this change might feel hard right now?

- If you decided not to change, what would your life look like?

- It seems like you have some concerns about changing. What do you think they are?

- What are some things you might need to feel ready to take the first step?

Envisioning Reasons For Change

- What kind of legacy do you want to leave behind?

- What would your life look like in five years if you made this change?

- What's something you're working toward that feels meaningful to you?

- What's the bigger picture for you, beyond this current challenge?

Beginning Steps For Change

- What's one small thing you could do this week to get closer to your goal?

- How will you handle obstacles if they come up during this process?

- What's the first step you'd feel comfortable taking toward change?

- What does success look like for you in the next month?

- If you had a plan, what would the first step look like?

Celebrating Progress

- What's one thing you've done recently that you feel good about?

- How does it feel to look back on the progress you've made so far?

- What's one positive change you've noticed, even if it feels small?

- How will you reward yourself for taking steps toward your goals?

- What's something you're proud of yourself for, no matter how small?

CHAPTER SEVENTEEN

Reflecting On Cravings And Urges Prompts

Cravings and urges are similar, but they're not quite the same. A craving is that deeper, more persistent pull toward alcohol. It lingers, sometimes for hours or even days, often tied to emotions, memories, or the body's dependence. An urge, on the other hand, is sharp and immediate. It hits in the moment—triggered by a familiar place, a stressful day, or even just seeing a drink in someone's hand. One simmers, the other strikes. While there's a distinction between the two, I'll use *cravings* and *urges* interchangeably throughout this book for clarity and ease of reading.

Exploring and Managing Cravings

- What do you notice in your body or mind when a craving starts to appear?
- What situations tend to trigger your cravings the most?
- What strategies have you used in the past to manage cravings, and how did they work?
- When you feel a craving, what's the first thing you usually do?
- What would it feel like to let the craving pass without acting on it?
- If you could ride out a craving successfully, how would you feel afterward?
- What could you do in the moment to distract yourself or shift your focus?
- How long do you think most cravings last? What might help you endure that time?
- What are some non-harmful ways to soothe yourself when a craving feels intense?
- What's one thing you can prepare ahead of time to help you manage cravings when they occur?

Building Awareness of Cravings

- How do your thoughts during a craving differ from how you feel afterward?
- What's the first sign that a craving is starting for you?
- Are there particular places or people that tend to amplify your cravings?
- What emotions often accompany your cravings?

☐ How do you think your cravings have changed over time, if at all?

Growing Capacity To Manage Cravings

☐ Can you recall a time when you successfully resisted a craving? What did you do?

☐ What strengths or tools helped you manage cravings in the past?

☐ If you were to rate your ability to handle cravings on a scale from 1 to 10, what number would you choose and why?

☐ What's one small action you can take today to increase your confidence in handling cravings?

☐ Who or what inspires you to believe in your ability to resist cravings?

Planning Ahead To Manage Cravings

☐ What's one activity you could do instead of giving in to a craving?

☐ How could reaching out to someone you trust help you when a craving arises?

☐ What's one step you could take to create a craving-free environment at home?

☐ What would a 'cravings toolkit' look like for you, and what would it include?

☐ How could practicing mindfulness or relaxation techniques help with cravings?

Exploring Beliefs About Cravings

☐ What do you believe about your cravings and your ability to manage them?

☐ What do you tell yourself during a craving, and how does it affect your actions?

☐ If cravings are temporary, what might help you stay focused on that idea?

☐ How does giving in to cravings fit with your long-term goals?

☐ What would you like to believe about yourself when it comes to managing cravings?

Navigating Cravings In The Habit Void

☐ What's one strength you've used in other challenges that could help you here?

☐ When have you successfully gotten through this time without drinking? What worked?

☐ What's something meaningful you could add to this time to make it feel less empty?

☐ How can you remind yourself why you're making this change when the urge hits?

☐ If you could give yourself encouragement in this moment, what would you say?

CHAPTER EIGHTEEN

Addressing Setbacks Prompts

Reframing Setbacks

☐ How can a setback be an opportunity to learn and grow stronger?

☐ What's one thing you've learned from past challenges that can help you now?

☐ How can you remind yourself that progress isn't always linear?

☐ What would you say to a friend who's feeling discouraged about a setback?

☐ How can you use what you've learned from this experience to make a different choice next time?

Visualizing Success

- [ ] If you succeeded in overcoming cravings consistently, how would you feel about yourself?
- [ ] What would it look like to take control over your cravings instead of the other way around?
- [ ] What kind of life do you want to build for yourself, and how does managing cravings help get you there?
- [ ] If someone else could see your progress, what do you think they'd be most proud of?
- [ ] What's one habit or action you could build that would make you feel stronger over time?

Building Confidence Through Actions

- [ ] What's a small but meaningful goal you can set for yourself this week?
- [ ] How would celebrating your successes, even small ones, help you stay motivated?
- [ ] What's one action you can take today that reinforces your belief in your ability to succeed?
- [ ] How can you practice self-compassion when things don't go as planned?
- [ ] What's one new skill or technique you'd like to learn to improve your confidence?

Exploring Resources and Support

□ Who in your life can remind you of your strengths when you feel unsure?

□ What resources, like support groups or online tools, could help you feel more capable?

□ How does being part of SMART Recovery inspire you to believe in your ability to change?

□ What's one way you can connect with others who are on a similar journey?

□ If you had a coach or cheerleader, what do you think they'd tell you right now?

Exploring Discrepancies

□ How does your current behavior align with your long-term goals?

□ What are some things you're missing out on because of this behavior?

□ How do you feel about where you are now compared to where you'd like to be?

Exploring Impact:

□ What effects has this behavior had on your relationships or other areas of your life?

□ How do you think things might look if you continue on this path?

□ What could be different in your life if you decided to change?

Reflective Practice Prompts

□ What did you hear yourself saying just now?

□ How does that realization feel to you?

□ What steps, if any, are you ready to take next?

CHAPTER NINETEEN

Handling Challenge And Change Prompts

Building Resilience

☐ What have you learned from past experiences about handling stress effectively?

☐ How do you recover from setbacks at work without letting them affect your recovery?

☐ What's one thing you can do to build your resilience in handling job demands?

☐ How do you reframe challenges at work as opportunities to grow?

☐ What's one resource or skill you'd like to develop to feel more confident at work?

Self-Care and Emotional Well-Being

☐ What self-care practices help you feel your best emotionally and physically?

☐ How do you know when you need to take a break or slow down?

☐ What's one thing you can do outside of work to recharge your energy?

☐ How do you balance your time between work, recovery, and personal life?

☐ What's something you've done recently to care for yourself, and how did it feel?

Physical Health and Energy

☐ How do you notice work stress affecting your body, like sleep, appetite, or energy?

☐ What's one small change to your daily routine that could help you feel more energized?

☐ Are there any physical activities you enjoy that help you feel balanced and healthy?

☐ How do you ensure you're eating well and staying hydrated during busy workdays?

☐ What's one way you can prioritize rest or relaxation, even on hectic days?

Goal Setting and Prioritization

☐ What's one goal you'd like to set to make work feel more manageable?

☐ How do you decide what's most important when you feel overwhelmed with tasks?

☐ What's a realistic step you can take to create a better balance between work and recovery?

☐ How can you break down big work challenges into smaller, more manageable pieces?

☐ What would success at work look like for you, without compromising your well-being?

Exploring Support Systems

☐ Who at work or outside of work could provide support when you're feeling overwhelmed?

☐ How comfortable do you feel discussing work-related stress with someone you trust?

☐ What's one way your support network can help you balance work and recovery?

☐ Are there any workplace resources, like an employee assistance program, you could use?

☐ How could connecting with others in recovery help you manage work stress?

Long-Term Vision

☐ How do you see your career benefiting your long-term recovery and well-being?

☐ What would an ideal balance between work, health, and recovery look like for you?

☐ What motivates you to keep moving forward, even when work feels challenging?

☐ How does staying in recovery support your ability to handle work stress?

☐ What's one thing you'd like to change about your current job situation to feel more aligned with your goals?

Problem-Solving and Action Planning

☐ What's one thing you can do today to make your workday feel less overwhelming?

☐ What's one problem you'd like to solve about your work-life balance, and how could you start?

☐ How can you prepare for particularly stressful workdays to stay on track with recovery?

☐ What's a simple relaxation or mindfulness technique you can use during your workday?

☐ How can you remind yourself to prioritize your well-being during busy times?

Maintaining Recovery

☐ How do you stay connected to your recovery goals when work feels overwhelming?

☐ What tools or practices help you maintain your recovery while managing job demands?

☐ How do you remind yourself of the progress you've made in recovery during tough times?

☐ What support systems can you rely on when work pressures feel too much?

☐ How can your recovery strengths, like resilience or self-awareness, help you manage work stress?

Exploring Everyday Stressors and Triggers

☐ What are some ways the stress has been affecting your thoughts or feelings lately?

☐ How does stress show up in your day-to-day life—physically, emotionally, or behaviorally?

☐ When you feel overwhelmed by stress, what thoughts or urges come up regarding your recovery?

☐ What do you notice about your triggers when the stress feels more intense?

☐ What helps you stay grounded when relationship stress starts to feel overwhelming?

Focusing on Self-Care

☐ What are some things you can do for yourself to manage stress in a healthy way?

☐ How do you take care of your physical and emotional health when you're feeling stretched thin?

☐ What's one self-care habit you've practiced in the past that could help you now?

☐ How could creating a routine for yourself help reduce some of the stress you're experiencing?

☐ What's something simple you could do each day to feel more balanced and in control?

Identifying Strengths and Resources

☐ What personal strengths have helped you stay in recovery so far, even when faced with stress?

☐ What resources or support systems could you lean on during this challenging time?

☐ How has your progress in recovery prepared you to handle situations like this?

☐ What past challenges have you overcome that can remind you of your resilience?

□ Who or what in your life gives you encouragement to keep moving forward?

Managing Emotional Responses

□ What do you notice about your emotions when stress builds up, and how do you handle them?

□ How do you typically react to conflict, and is there a way to respond that feels healthier for you?

□ What could you do to calm yourself before reacting when emotions are running high?

□ What helps you create space to process difficult emotions without turning to unhealthy habits?

□ If stress feels unmanageable, how could you remind yourself of the tools you've learned in recovery?

Staying Focused on Recovery Goals

□ What's your ultimate goal for staying on track with your recovery, even during tough times?

□ How does staying in recovery help you show up as your best self in stressful situations?

□ What motivates you to stay committed to your recovery, despite the challenges you're facing?

- How could a slip or relapse make the current situation more complicated for you?
- What strategies have you developed to stay focused on your recovery when life feels out of control?

Strengthening Healthy Coping Skills

- What's one coping skill you've learned in recovery that you could use to manage stress today?
- How do activities like exercise, journaling, or mindfulness help you during tough times?
- What role does relaxation or breathing techniques play in keeping you grounded?
- When you feel the urge to escape stress, what could you do instead to feel better?
- How could practicing gratitude or focusing on positives help you shift your perspective?

Planning for Challenging Moments

- What's a potential stressor you see coming up, and how could you plan for it?
- How do you remind yourself of your recovery plan when stress starts to rise?

- What's one thing you could do to create a safety net for yourself during particularly difficult days?
- How do you balance the need to address your stress with the need to prioritize your recovery?
- What's something you could practice or prepare ahead of time to help you manage urges?

Cultivating Self-Empowerment

- What's one small action you could take today to feel more in control of your recovery?
- How do you remind yourself that you have the power to choose your response to stress?
- What does it mean to you to take ownership of your own emotional well-being?
- How can focusing on what you can control help you feel less overwhelmed by what you can't?
- What does success in your recovery look like for you, even in the face of stress?

Building Long-Term Resilience

- How could staying committed to your recovery help strengthen your resilience in other areas of life?

☐ What lessons have you learned about yourself through the challenges you've faced in recovery?

☐ What's something you could start practicing now to help you feel prepared for future stressors?

☐ How do you see yourself growing through this experience, both in recovery and in life?

Exploring Past Experiences to Build Resilience

☐ What is an unexpected challenge you've faced in the past, and how did you manage to get through it?

☐ What strengths or skills did you use during a tough time that helped you cope effectively?

☐ What's a time you dealt with a stressful event better than you expected, and why do you think that was?

☐ What's a challenge you faced before that seemed impossible at the time but taught you something valuable?

☐ How have you surprised yourself in handling unexpected difficulties in the past?

☐ What role did support from others play in helping you get through past challenges?

☐ What's one lesson you've learned from a difficult situation that you still use today?

☐ When have you felt proud of how you handled a tough or unexpected event?

□ What coping tools or methods worked well for you in the past, and how could you use them now?

□ What's an event from your past that helps you feel more confident about facing the future?

Identifying Current Coping Strategies

□ What are some strategies you currently use to manage stress or difficult emotions?

□ What's something you do now that helps you stay calm and focused in stressful situations?

□ How do you create space for yourself to think and plan when stress is high?

□ What's an activity or ritual you rely on to feel more grounded during tough times?

□ When you feel stressed, what's one small action you take to bring yourself back to balance?

□ What's one thing you already know how to do that helps you handle stress effectively?

□ How do you know when it's time to pause and use a coping tool or technique?

Highlighting Strengths:

- What strengths or skills do you have that could help you make a change?
- Can you think of a time when you overcame a challenge? How did you do it?
- What are some small steps you could take toward your goals?

Exploring Support Systems:

- Who in your life could support you as you work on this?
- What role would you like your friends or family to play in your journey?
- How could reaching out for support help you in this process?

Building Confidence

- What gives you confidence that you can make this change?
- If you were to succeed, how would you know you're making progress?
- What's a small, manageable change you feel ready to try this week?

CHAPTER TWENTY

Planning For Life's Curveballs Prompts

Preparing for Unpredictable Events

☐ If a stressful event happened tomorrow, what steps could you take to stay grounded?

☐ What kind of plan could you create for yourself to handle unexpected challenges?

☐ What's one skill or habit you could develop now to help you face the unexpected?

☐ How do you usually react to sudden changes or surprises, and how might you want to adjust those reactions?

☐ What's something you could practice now to prepare yourself for future stressful situations?

☐ What does it mean to you to be ready for the unexpected?

- What's one thing you can control in your life, even when everything else feels uncertain?
- How could you adapt your current recovery plan to include strategies for unexpected stress?

Developing Emotional Regulation Skills

- When stress hits, how do you remind yourself to take a step back before reacting?
- What helps you stay calm when your emotions start to feel overwhelming?
- What techniques could you practice now, like deep breathing or mindfulness, to use in future stressful moments?
- How do you process emotions like frustration, anger, or sadness in healthy ways?
- What's one thing you could tell yourself during a stressful event to help you stay focused and resilient?
- How could practicing mindfulness or meditation help you manage difficult emotions?
- What do you notice about your body or mind when stress starts to build up?
- How can you use relaxation techniques to shift your focus when emotions run high?
- What's a grounding exercise you could practice now to prepare for future challenges?

☐ How do you give yourself permission to pause and check in with your emotions?

Building Problem-Solving Skills

☐ How do you approach problems when they feel too big or overwhelming?

☐ What's a strategy you've used to break down a challenge into smaller, more manageable steps?

☐ When faced with a difficult decision, how do you weigh your options and choose the best path forward?

☐ What's one thing you could practice to improve your ability to solve problems under stress?

☐ What resources or tools could you rely on to help you find solutions during challenging times?

☐ How do you stay focused on solutions instead of getting stuck on the problem?

☐ What's an example of a creative solution you've come up with in the past?

☐ How do you remind yourself to focus on what you can do in stressful situations?

☐ What steps could you take to turn a stressful situation into an opportunity to learn?

☐ How do you balance quick thinking with careful planning when solving problems?

Strengthening Support Networks

☐ Who in your life could you turn to for support when unexpected challenges arise?

☐ How do you build and maintain relationships with people who can be a source of encouragement and guidance?

☐ What role does your support network play in helping you cope with stress?

☐ How could you strengthen your connections with others to feel more supported in the future?

☐ What's one way you could ask for help or support when you need it during tough times?

☐ Who inspires or motivates you to keep going when life gets hard?

☐ What's a simple way to let others know you might need their support during difficult times?

☐ How do you remind yourself that asking for help is a sign of strength, not weakness?

☐ What's one thing you could do to show appreciation for the support you've received?

☐ How do you decide who to lean on for help when challenges arise?

Focusing on Personal Growth and Mindset

☐ What does it mean to you to be resilient in the face of unexpected challenges?

- How do you remind yourself that challenges can also be opportunities for growth?
- What's a positive mindset or affirmation you could practice to help you stay strong during stressful events?
- How do you focus on what you can control, even when some things feel completely out of your hands?
- What helps you stay hopeful or optimistic, even in difficult situations?
- How could changing your perspective on stress help you see it in a different light?
- What's a past experience where you grew as a person because of a challenge?
- How could focusing on gratitude help you stay centered during tough times?
- What do you think it means to turn a setback into a setup for something better?
- What's one way to remind yourself of your purpose or values when stress feels overwhelming?

Creating a Plan for the Future

- What's one thing you could do now to prepare yourself for unexpected challenges in the future?
- How could creating a self-care routine help you stay resilient when life gets tough?

□ What are some signs that you might need to slow down and focus on your well-being during stressful times?

□ How could practicing flexibility or adaptability help you handle life's surprises?

□ What's one resource or tool you could have on hand to help you navigate future stressors?

□ What's a plan you could put into place to help you feel more confident about handling stress?

□ How do you balance staying prepared with staying present in the moment?

□ What steps could you take to ensure you're prioritizing your well-being in the future?

□ How do you remind yourself of the importance of long-term thinking when stress hits?

□ What's one practice or habit you could adopt now to strengthen your resilience for the future?

Building Confidence and Self-Empowerment

□ What does it mean to you to take control of your own response to stress?

□ How do you remind yourself of your inner strength and ability to handle tough situations?

□ What's one way you can practice trusting yourself to make good decisions under pressure?

- What's something you've achieved that proves you're capable of overcoming challenges?
- How do you see yourself becoming stronger and more resilient through this process?
- How could practicing self-compassion help you feel more empowered during stressful times?
- What's a mantra or phrase you could use to encourage yourself when life feels hard?
- How do you remind yourself of the progress you've already made in handling stress?
- What does being in control of your recovery and well-being mean to you?
- How do you focus on your ability to create change in your life, even during tough times?

Developing Healthy Outlets and Coping Skills

- What's an activity or hobby you could turn to when stress feels overwhelming?
- How does physical activity or exercise help you release tension or cope with stress?
- What creative outlets, like journaling or art, could you use to process your emotions?
- What role does humor or lightheartedness play in helping you cope with tough situations?

☐ How could practicing gratitude or focusing on the positives help you during stressful times?

☐ What's one self-soothing activity you've found helpful in managing stress?

☐ How could spending time in nature or outdoors help you feel more at ease?

☐ What role does music, reading, or other calming activities play in your stress relief?

☐ How could creating a list of calming activities help you prepare for unexpected stress?

☐ What's one small thing you could do today to strengthen your coping skills for the future?

CHAPTER TWENTY-ONE

Staying Motivated By Positive Changes Prompts

Understanding Alcohol's Impact on Sleep and Restorative Processes

☐ Looking back, how do you feel about the quality of your sleep when you were drinking compared to now that you're sober? How does a good night's sleep impact your energy and mood?

☐ Now that you're experiencing better sleep in recovery, how does that make you feel about the potential long-term benefits of staying sober?

☐ How have you noticed your overall health improving since you stopped drinking, particularly when it comes to rest and mental clarity?

□ Reflecting on the way alcohol disrupted your sleep, how important do you think it is to maintain healthy sleep patterns moving forward in your recovery?

□ How does waking up feeling rested and clear-minded now compare to your experiences in the past when alcohol impacted your sleep? How does that motivate you to stay alcohol-free?

Exploring the Influence of Alcohol on GABA and Its Effects on the Body

□ How does it feel to recognize that alcohol may have made it harder for you to stay calm or relaxed in the past, and how does that change how you view your current ability to manage stress without alcohol?

□ In what ways has your ability to cope with stress or emotional challenges improved since you've been sober, and how does that make you feel about your future without alcohol?

□ How do you feel knowing that alcohol's impact on GABA may have influenced your emotional stability in the past, and how does the absence of alcohol now allow you to feel more in control?

□ What have you noticed about your ability to stay calm and emotionally balanced in situations that used to be difficult when you drank? How does this strengthen your commitment to staying sober?

□ How would you describe the sense of relief you feel from no longer needing alcohol to relax, and how might this positively affect your long-term emotional health?

Dopamine and Emotional Well-being: The Cycle of Reward and Depletion

□ Looking back, how do you feel alcohol may have affected your ability to enjoy the things you once loved, and how does it feel to find that joy again in sobriety?

□ How does experiencing more stable emotions in recovery make you feel about the potential for a healthier and more balanced life moving forward without alcohol?

□ Reflecting on how alcohol impacted your sense of reward and pleasure, how would you describe the positive changes you've noticed now that you're sober?

□ What are some of the things that bring you genuine pleasure and motivation in your sober life, and how do those experiences compare to the temporary highs alcohol once gave you?

□ How does it feel to recognize that your emotional and physical well-being is no longer being depleted by alcohol, and how does that give you more hope for a brighter future in recovery?

Recognizing Alcohol's Snowball Effect on Health and Emotional Well-being

□ How have you noticed your physical health improving since stopping drinking, and how does that motivate you to continue making healthier choices for your body?

□ Reflecting on the negative emotional impact alcohol had on you in the past, how does it feel to have a clearer, more stable emotional state now that you're sober?

□ What positive changes have you noticed in your emotional health since you stopped drinking, and how do those changes influence your determination to remain alcohol-free?

□ How do you feel about the long-term benefits of maintaining sobriety for your overall well-being, both physically and emotionally?

□ When you think about your health and emotional state without alcohol, how does this reinforce your commitment to a life free from alcohol?

Reflecting on the Cycle of Drinking and Recovery

□ Looking back at the cycle of alcohol use and its consequences, how does it feel to break free from that cycle and experience life without those negative effects?

□ How does staying sober allow you to handle stress or difficult emotions more effectively, and what does that tell you about the long-term benefits of living alcohol-free?

□ Reflecting on the way alcohol used to affect your body and mind, how do you feel about the positive changes you're experiencing now that you are sober?

□ What does it feel like to face life's challenges without alcohol, and how does that make you feel more capable and empowered in your recovery?

□ How do you think your future will look as you continue to experience life without the negative impacts of alcohol, and how does that vision strengthen your desire to stay sober for good?

Exploring Progress and Growth

□ What's one thing you're most proud of since starting your recovery journey again?

□ How have things changed for you in the last few months?

□ What have you learned about yourself during this recovery period?

□ What's working well for you this time that's different from before?

□ What positive changes have you noticed in your relationships or daily life?

Reinforcing Commitment

□ What keeps you motivated to stay on track with your recovery?

□ What are the biggest reasons you're committed to this journey?

□ How does staying in recovery align with the person you want to be?

□ What's something you're looking forward to in your recovery?

□ What would you say to your past self to encourage them to keep going?

Reflecting on Lessons from Relapse

☐ What did your relapse teach you about what you need to stay successful in recovery?

☐ What's one thing you'd like to do differently if you face challenges again?

☐ How has your perspective on relapse changed since then?

☐ What support systems have you put in place to reduce the risk of future relapses?

☐ How can you use your experiences to help others who might be struggling?

Building Confidence and Resilience

☐ What's something you've done recently that shows how resilient you are?

☐ When you face challenges now, how do you handle them differently than before?

☐ What's one area of your recovery where you feel really strong?

☐ How do you remind yourself of your ability to overcome setbacks?

☐ What would your future self say about the progress you're making right now?

Identifying and Overcoming Challenges

□ What's been the most challenging part of the last few months, and how did you handle it?

□ Are there any habits or triggers that you're still working to manage?

□ How do you cope when you're feeling stressed or tempted?

□ What's a challenge you overcame recently, and what did you learn from it?

□ What resources or support do you think could help you continue to strengthen your recovery?

Maintaining Momentum

□ What daily habits or routines help you stay focused on your recovery?

□ What's one goal you'd like to work toward in the next few months?

□ How do you plan to celebrate milestones in your recovery journey?

□ What's a small step you can take today to keep building your momentum?

□ What's something you've done in the past few months that you never thought you'd be able to do?

Reinforcing Support Systems

□ Who has been most supportive during this recovery period, and how have they helped you?

□ What role does your support network play in your recovery right now?

□ How do you stay connected to others who are also focused on recovery?

□ What's one thing you can do to strengthen your support system?

□ How do you reach out for help when you're feeling uncertain or vulnerable?

Focusing on Self-Care

□ What's something you do regularly to take care of yourself emotionally or physically?

□ How do you balance recovery with other areas of your life?

□ What's one new activity or practice you've discovered that brings you joy?

□ How do you practice self-compassion when things don't go as planned?

□ What's one way you've been kind to yourself recently?

Future-Focused Prompts

□ Where do you see yourself in six months if you continue on this path?

☐ What's a long-term goal you're excited to achieve in your recovery?

☐ How do you envision your life looking as you continue to grow in your recovery?

☐ What's one thing you'd like to achieve in the next year that feels meaningful to you?

☐ If you could give someone else advice based on your experiences, what would you say?

Celebrating Success

☐ What's the biggest accomplishment you've achieved during this recovery period?

☐ How do you feel when you think about how far you've come?

☐ What's one thing you've done that you thought would be impossible a few months ago?

☐ How can you reward yourself for the progress you've made?

☐ What's a reminder you can use to celebrate your successes daily?

CHAPTER TWENTY-TWO

Learning From Past Relapses Prompts

Exploring the Underlying Causes of Past Relapses

☐ Can you think of any patterns or situations that led to your relapses in the past?

☐ Were there signs in your body or feelings that you ignored before relapsing? How might noticing them earlier have helped?

☐ What was going on in your mind or emotions just before you relapsed? What could you have done to handle those feelings differently?

☐ When you think back to your relapses, what life stress or emotions were affecting you, and how can you deal with them differently next time?

- How did your own expectations about staying sober affect your choices? How can you adjust those expectations to stay on track?
- Think about the times you didn't relapse—what helped you stay strong? How can you use that strength in the future?
- How did alcohol or your old habits help you avoid feelings? How can you start dealing with those feelings in a healthier way?

Understanding Emotional and Mental Triggers

- How do you think your emotions like stress or anxiety led to your relapses before?
- Can you remember any specific emotions or situations that pushed you toward relapsing?
- What healthy ways can you handle those emotions without using alcohol?
- How do you notice when you're starting to feel off-track, and what can you do to stop yourself from going down the path of relapse?
- Looking back, what made you feel like drinking was the solution? What can you do next time to make a healthier choice?
- Alcohol affected how you felt in the past. How can you start meeting those emotional needs without alcohol?

Reflecting on Social and Environmental Influences

☐ How have your friends, family, or social settings affected your relapses? What can you change to protect your recovery in the future?

☐ Were there certain people or places that made you want to drink? How can you avoid or set limits with them?

☐ When you've been around people or situations where alcohol was present, how did you respond? What can you do differently to stay sober?

☐ When alcohol is around, how do you feel? What can you do to stay true to your recovery in those situations?

☐ How can you surround yourself with people or places that support your recovery?

Exploring the Impact of Negative Thinking and Self-Doubt

☐ How do you think negative thoughts about yourself and your recovery affected past relapses?

☐ When you doubt yourself or your ability to stay sober, how can you remind yourself of how far you've come?

☐ How do you deal with feelings of failure or disappointment? How can you use those feelings to stay committed to your recovery instead of giving up?

□ Looking back, did unrealistic expectations of yourself play a role in relapsing? How can you change your expectations to help yourself stay sober?

□ How do you define success in recovery? What small goals can you set to keep yourself on track without feeling overwhelmed?

□ Have you ever felt like you weren't doing well enough? How did that affect your choices, and how can you be kinder to yourself in the future?

Building Strategies for Long-Term Sobriety

□ What steps can you take now to make sure you're prepared for challenges ahead?

□ How do you feel about having tools ready to use when stress or temptation hits? What tools do you think could help?

□ Before you relapsed, were there smaller choices or feelings that led to it? How can you catch those early next time?

□ What positive changes have you noticed in your life since staying sober? How can you build on those?

□ How do you feel about being prepared for future challenges instead of waiting for them to happen? What can you do now to be ready?

□ Do you feel confident in staying sober in the future? What strengths do you have that can help you stay on track?

Strengthening Resilience and Commitment to Sobriety

☐ How can you use your past experiences to build a stronger, more resilient recovery?

☐ When you face tough days, how can you remind yourself of the strength it took to get this far?

☐ How can you make staying sober part of your daily routine so it feels normal, not like a struggle?

☐ What keeps you going on tough days? How can you use that motivation to stay sober for good?

☐ How does it feel when you recognize how far you've come in your recovery? How does that help you stay committed to sobriety?

☐ What positive changes have you seen in your life since becoming sober, and how can you keep making progress?

Recognizing and Managing Relapse Risks in Real-Time

☐ When you're stressed, how can you slow down and check in with yourself to see if you're headed toward a relapse?

☐ How can you notice when you're feeling disconnected from your recovery, and what can you do to get back on track?

☐ Who or what can you turn to when you start feeling like you might relapse?

☐ When you feel disconnected from your recovery, what healthy distractions or calming techniques can help you stay focused?

☐ How can you learn to understand how your emotions, thoughts, and body are connected to avoid relapse in the future?

CHAPTER TWENTY-THREE

Navigating Emotional Upsets Prompts

Exploring Emotional Triggers And Potential for Relapse

☐ What's the strongest emotion you're feeling right now, and how do you think it might affect your decisions moving forward?

☐ How does it feel to recognize that your emotions may be pushing you toward past behaviors that you've worked to avoid?

☐ When you think about how this emotional upset is affecting you, do you notice any changes in how you're thinking about your recovery?

☐ How can you respond to this situation in a way that respects your emotional needs, without letting it take you off track in your recovery?

- What part of the interaction feels like it's causing the biggest emotional impact for you? How can you handle it in a way that protects your recovery?
- How do you think this emotional pain could be affecting your motivation to continue working on your recovery?
- What do you think it might look like to manage this emotional upset without letting it create a setback in your journey?
- How does this emotional situation align with past patterns that have challenged your ability to stay sober or on track with recovery?
- When emotional discomfort arises, how do you remind yourself that it's just one moment, not the whole story of your recovery?
- How do you typically respond to emotional triggers like this—do you feel like it might be harder to stick to healthy coping mechanisms?
- What do you notice about your thinking when you feel upset—do you find yourself questioning your ability to stay on the path?
- How can you take responsibility for your emotions, but also ensure that they don't take away from your commitment to staying sober?
- What's one small action you can take today to break the cycle of emotional reaction and stay focused on your recovery?
- How can you use this moment to reinforce your emotional resilience, knowing that it won't define your recovery journey?
- How do you remind yourself that these emotions don't need to control your actions in a way that could harm your recovery?
- How does recognizing your emotional response help you stay in control, and avoid allowing it to derail your recovery?

Addressing the Connection Between Emotional Pain and Relapse Risks

☐ When you feel emotional pain, do you notice if it changes your perspective on how you're doing with your recovery?

☐ How do you think this emotional upset might influence your ability to stay on track with your long-term recovery goals?

☐ What do you think might help you manage this emotional distress without letting it negatively affect your recovery path?

☐ What strategies could you use to process this emotional discomfort without feeling overwhelmed or tempted to relapse?

☐ How can you use this emotional experience to reflect on your progress, and also stay committed to your recovery goals?

☐ How can you shift your mindset in moments like this to stay focused on your journey, even when emotions feel heavy?

☐ What would it take for you to stay focused on recovery, despite feeling hurt or upset by what was said?

☐ How do you feel about acknowledging these emotions without letting them stop you from moving forward in your recovery?

☐ What are some healthy coping skills that could help you release this emotional tension, so it doesn't influence your recovery?

☐ What helps you return to a place of calm when emotions feel overwhelming, so that they don't interfere with your recovery?

□ How can you remind yourself that this emotional upset is temporary, and won't define your ability to stay on track?

□ What helps you shift your perspective when you feel triggered by a situation or interaction, so you can stay focused on your progress?

□ When you're dealing with emotional pain, what steps do you think could help prevent it from hindering your recovery?

□ What would help you reclaim your emotional balance in moments like these, without losing sight of your recovery goals?

□ How can you take control of your emotional state when it starts to feel like it could lead you away from your recovery?

□ When you feel hurt or upset, how can you give yourself permission to process the emotion without it taking over your journey?

□ How do you stay empowered to protect your recovery when emotional distress tries to influence your actions?

□ What do you think it takes to honor your feelings, but still prioritize your recovery in moments like this?

□ When emotional discomfort arises, how do you practice patience with yourself while staying committed to your recovery?

□ What would it look like to be gentle with yourself during emotional stress, while ensuring it doesn't steer you away from your goals?

Exploring Emotional Awareness in the Moment

□ How can you manage moments like this when emotional upset feels like it could pull you away from your recovery goals?

☐ When you reflect on this, do you notice old behaviors or feelings resurfacing that could potentially lead you down a familiar path?

☐ How does your body feel right now as you think about what was said? Does it affect how you feel about your recovery progress?

☐ What would it take for you to be gentle with yourself right now, while still keeping your long-term recovery goals in mind?

☐ How can you separate your emotional response from the need to make choices that support your recovery today?

☐ What strategies can you use to avoid letting your emotional reactions cloud your judgment in this moment?

☐ How do you feel about your emotional state right now? How might it lead you away from what you've worked so hard for in your recovery?

☐ What would it look like to take a moment to pause and check in with yourself, when you feel emotionally affected by someone's words?

☐ When you experience emotional upset, what do you think it would look like to respond in a way that's aligned with your recovery?

☐ What do you think it takes for you to process your emotions without allowing them to negatively affect your recovery path?

☐ When emotions like these come up, how do you remind yourself of the bigger picture of your recovery?

☐ What would it look like to protect your recovery, even while acknowledging that you're feeling emotionally affected by the situation?

Cultivating Self-Awareness and Growth

☐ What have you learned about your own emotions from this situation?

☐ Looking back, what do you think you can do differently next time to manage how you feel?

☐ What would help you shift your perspective when someone happens that is upsetting?

☐ How can you stay focused on what's in your control when others make comments that upset you?

☐ How do you turn situations like this into opportunities for growth, both emotionally and in your recovery?

Exploring Self-Compassion and Awareness

☐ How can you show yourself kindness when you're feeling upset, so that it doesn't impact your recovery journey?

☐ What would it feel like to acknowledge the discomfort you're feeling without letting it take you off course in your recovery?

☐ How can you remind yourself that it's okay to feel hurt, but it's also important to protect your progress and self-care?

☐ When you feel pain or discomfort, how can you focus on taking care of yourself in ways that prevent relapse?

□ What's one healthy thing you can do right now to help soothe the
emotional discomfort you're feeling without letting it lead you
down a path you don't want to go down?

□ How do you remind yourself that this moment of emotional pain is
just *a moment* and doesn't have to define your recovery path?

□ When you notice that you're hurt or upset, how can you check in
with yourself to make sure you're staying on track with what
matters most to you?

□ How can you give yourself space to feel your emotions while still
keeping your recovery goals at the forefront?

□ What can you do to prevent emotional hurt from becoming an
excuse to avoid the hard work you've committed to in recovery?

□ How do you stay aware of the connection between your emotional
health and your recovery, even when things feel difficult?

CHAPTER TWENTY-FOUR

Acceptance Of What Is Prompts

Exploring Self-Compassion and Awareness

☐ When you feel emotional distress, how do you gently remind yourself that it's okay to feel, but you can also stay focused on your goals?

☐ How can you acknowledge your emotional pain without letting it stop you from moving forward in your recovery?

☐ How do you practice self-compassion in moments like this, when your emotions feel overwhelming and could potentially impact your progress?

☐ What would it look like to recognize your emotional discomfort without letting it overshadow the positive steps you've made in your recovery?

- How do you balance emotional self-care and recovery goals when they seem to conflict with each other?
- What kind of reminder or affirmation could you give yourself when emotions like this arise, to avoid getting stuck in negative thinking?
- What is one thing you can do to remind yourself that your recovery deserves your attention, even when emotions feel heavy?
- How do you create space for yourself to process difficult emotions, while still ensuring you're moving forward in your recovery?
- When you're emotionally overwhelmed, how can you reassure yourself that these feelings won't define the next step in your recovery?
- How do you notice your emotional responses impacting your confidence in your recovery—what steps can you take to reset that mindset?
- What do you need to hear from yourself to feel empowered to move through this emotional moment and stay on course with your recovery?
- How can you use self-compassion to shift your thinking when you're emotionally distressed, so you don't lose sight of your recovery goals?
- How do you separate your emotional pain from your need to stay focused on your long-term recovery journey?
- What's one thing you can do right now to protect your emotional health while honoring your commitment to recovery?

- How can you remind yourself that you have the ability to process your emotions, without letting them take control of your actions?
- What do you think it takes to honor your feelings, but still prioritize your recovery in moments like this?
- When faced with emotional pain, how can you reframe it as an opportunity to strengthen your emotional resilience and protect your recovery?
- How do you create a buffer between your emotional reactions and the decisions you make regarding your recovery?
- When emotional discomfort arises, how can you reframe it as a moment to practice emotional resilience and safeguard your recovery?

Unconditional Self-Acceptance

- How do you decide how much time and energy to give to others?
- What happens when you put others' needs ahead of your own for long periods of time?
- How do you typically respond to yourself when you feel tired or overwhelmed?
- When was the last time you took a moment to focus on what you need? How did that feel?
- What helps you recognize when it's time to slow down or take care of yourself?

- How do you think your life might change if you prioritized your well-being more often?
- How do you know when you've given enough in a situation?
- When you feel frustrated or unappreciated, what do you think you need most in that moment?
- What are some ways you can celebrate your efforts and progress without needing validation from others?
- How do you think setting boundaries could help you stay balanced and effective in your relationships or work?
- What do you notice about how your emotions change when you focus on a problem for a long time?
- How do you take care of yourself when small challenges start to feel overwhelming?
- When you feel frustrated or upset, how do you usually decide what to do next?
- What would it feel like to remind yourself that it's okay to make mistakes or not have all the answers?
- How can you begin to notice when a problem is taking more of your energy than it needs to?
- What helps you bring your focus back to what's most important when something feels urgent?
- How do you usually balance addressing a problem with giving yourself time to pause and reflect?
- What would it look like to be as patient with yourself as you would with someone you care about?
- When you feel a strong reaction to something, what helps you take a step back before responding?

☐ How do you usually feel after a situation where emotions run high?

Unconditional Acceptance of Others

☐ How do you usually respond when someone doesn't meet your expectations?

☐ What helps you understand where others might be coming from, even if their actions frustrate you?

☐ When someone doesn't give back in the way you hoped, how do you make sense of that?

☐ How do you think letting go of expectations for others might affect your stress levels?

☐ What do you think could make it easier to focus on what others do contribute, rather than what's missing?

☐ How do you remind yourself that everyone has their own challenges and limitations?

☐ What might help you approach others with more patience or understanding when they fall short?

☐ How do you think your relationships might change if you worked on accepting others as they are?

☐ What would it look like to balance holding people accountable with understanding their circumstances?

☐ How can you focus on the positives in a relationship, even when it feels one-sided?

☐ How do you usually respond when someone does something that feels frustrating or inconsiderate?

- What might help you understand why someone acted the way they did, even if it doesn't make sense at first?
- How do you decide whether to speak up about something that bothers you or to let it go?
- What helps you remember that others might not always see things the same way you do?
- How might it feel to give someone the benefit of the doubt, even if their actions hurt you?
- When someone reacts in a way that surprises you, what helps you stay calm and open-minded?
- How can you remind yourself that people have different ways of handling stress or challenges?
- What might happen if you tried to focus on understanding others rather than expecting them to change?
- How do you think relationships could grow if you focused more on connection than on solving every issue?
- How might letting go of expectations for others help you feel more at peace?

Connecting Self-Acceptance and Acceptance of Others

- When you feel frustrated with someone, how do you decide whether to adjust your expectations or communicate your feelings?
- How do you think accepting your own limitations could make it easier to accept others'?

- What helps you notice when your feelings about someone else's actions are tied to unmet needs of your own?
- How can you tell when your own feelings or experiences are shaping the way you view someone else?
- What would it feel like to focus more on connection and understanding than on fairness or equality?
- How might learning to be kinder to yourself change the way you interact with others?
- What happens when you focus more on the things you value in yourself than on how others respond to you?
- How can you approach moments of conflict or frustration in a way that strengthens your relationships?
- What do you think could help you feel more secure in relationships, even when others don't respond as you'd like?
- How do you think balancing self-care with care for others might improve both your well-being and your relationships?
- When you feel stuck on a problem, how do you think that might affect the way you see others?
- How do you know when a situation is worth pursuing or when it's time to let it go?
- What helps you notice when your own emotions might be influencing how you see someone else's actions?
- How might forgiving yourself for being upset make it easier to understand someone else's perspective?
- What happens when you focus on calming yourself before responding to others?

- How could practicing patience with yourself also help you approach others more calmly?
- How might understanding your own feelings help you communicate more clearly with others?
- When conflict arises, what can you do to stay grounded and avoid reacting too quickly?
- How can focusing on your own progress help you let go of frustrations with others?
- What would it look like to focus on building trust and understanding, even after a difficult moment?

Developing the Skill to Let Go

- When something doesn't go as planned, what helps you decide if it's worth holding onto?
- How do you feel when you've spent a lot of energy thinking about a problem? Does it help or make things harder?
- What might it feel like to let go of a situation that's causing frustration or stress?
- How do you decide when it's better to focus on solutions versus stepping back from a situation?
- When you're holding onto a negative feeling, what do you notice about how it affects your day?
- What are some small things you could practice letting go of to see how it feels?

- How can you tell when your thoughts about a situation are helping versus when they're making things harder?
- What would it look like to remind yourself that it's okay to let some things be as they are?
- How do you usually feel after you've been able to let go of something that bothered you?
- What could you do in the future when you notice yourself getting stuck on a problem or frustration?
- What would it feel like to let go of the need to address something and focus on what brings you peace instead?
- How can you remind yourself that some situations might resolve without your direct involvement?
- What might happen if you allowed yourself to step back from a situation, even if it feels unfinished?
- How can you tell when holding onto a concern is taking more energy than it's worth?
- What would letting go of a minor frustration allow you to focus on instead?
- How do you think your relationships might shift if you practiced letting go of smaller concerns?
- How do you decide whether a situation is worth addressing or if it's better for your well-being to let it go?
- What small step could you take today to practice letting go of a frustration or concern?
- How do you feel when you're able to let go of something that's been bothering you?

- What might happen if you gave yourself more time before deciding how to respond to something upsetting?
- When you think about holding onto frustrations, what impact does that have on your well-being?
- How might letting go of a small frustration free up your energy for something that matters more to you?
- What would it feel like to focus on your own peace in moments when you feel the urge to speak out?
- How do you think your relationships might grow if you practiced letting go of smaller concerns?
- What could help you recognize when holding onto a concern is no longer helping you?

CHAPTER TWENTY-FIVE

Regulating Emotional Responses Prompts

Reducing Interpersonal Harm

□ When you feel upset with someone, what helps you pause before responding?

□ How do you think the other person might feel when emotions are high on both sides?

□ What might happen if you took a step back before addressing a conflict or frustration?

□ How do you decide what's most important to say in a heated moment?

□ What are some ways you can show patience or understanding, even if you're upset?

- When you've been able to avoid reacting too quickly, how did it feel afterward?
- How do you think your relationships might change if you focused more on staying calm during conflicts?
- What helps you notice when you're holding onto something that could lead to a misunderstanding or harm?
- How can you shift your focus to repairing or improving a relationship instead of focusing on what went wrong?
- What would it look like to focus on kindness or forgiveness in a situation where you feel hurt?

Protecting Sobriety Through Letting Go

- How do you think holding onto negative emotions could affect your sobriety over time?
- What happens to your stress levels when you dwell on a problem for too long?
- How do you think letting go of frustrations could help you stay focused on your recovery?
- When you feel overwhelmed, what helps you reconnect with your goals for staying sober?
- How can you remind yourself that holding onto stress or anger might make it harder to stay balanced?
- What would it feel like to let go of something stressful and focus on what's going well in your life?

- How do you usually respond to emotional discomfort? What could you try that might work better for you?
- What's one small step you could take today to release a worry or frustration?
- How do you think your recovery journey might improve if you practiced letting go more often?
- When a stressful moment passes, what can you do to reinforce the importance of staying sober?

Exploring the Need to Assert

- When you feel strongly about addressing a situation, what makes it feel important to speak up?
- How do you usually feel after you've strongly asserted yourself to someone? Does it bring relief or something else?
- What do you think the other person might feel when you express your frustrations or concerns strongly?
- How do you decide when it's the right time to address a perceived wrong, and when it might be better to pause?
- What are some other ways you could communicate your thoughts without feeling the need to correct or challenge the other person?
- How do you know when your need to address an issue has been fully resolved, both emotionally and mentally?
- What might it feel like to let go of the need to address every concern and focus on your own peace instead?

- How does it affect your relationships when you feel the need to tell someone how you see things?
- When you assert yourself to correct a perceived wrong, what are you hoping to achieve?
- What feels most important to you when you decide to address something that doesn't sit right with you?
- How do you usually feel inside after expressing your thoughts about a situation that concerns you?
- When you think about times you've spoken up, what were you hoping the other person would understand about you or the situation?
- How do you think people receive your words when you share your perspective?
- What does it feel like when someone listens to your concerns? How does that compare to when they don't?
- What helps you decide when it's worth addressing a concern and when it might be okay to let it go?
- If you paused before responding to something upsetting, what do you think you might notice in yourself or the situation?

Identifying the Underlying Emotions

- How do you usually feel inside when you notice something that feels unjust or wrong?
- What might those feelings be telling you about what you value or need in that moment?

- When you think about the situations where you feel the strongest need to speak up, what patterns do you notice?
- How do you think your emotions might be influencing your actions in those moments?
- What do you notice about the intensity of your feelings before, during, and after you've spoken up?
- If you didn't address the situation right away, what emotions do you think might come up for you?
- What helps you feel more grounded when strong emotions start to take over?
- How might giving yourself a moment to reflect before acting change the way you feel about the situation?
- What do you feel most strongly when you notice something that feels unfair or wrong?
- When something really bothers you, what helps you understand what's happening inside you in that moment?
- How do you think your emotions might be guiding your actions when something doesn't feel right?
- When you think back to moments when you felt frustrated or upset, what stands out most about how you felt?
- How do you feel when you've taken some time to think about a situation before acting?
- What might you learn about yourself if you explored the emotions behind your reactions?
- How do you know when your emotions are leading you toward something constructive versus something that might cause hurt?

Protecting Emotional and Relational Balance

☐ When you assert yourself in a strong way, how does it affect the trust and connection in your relationships?

☐ How do you think your actions might be interpreted by others, even when your intentions are good?

☐ What would it look like to communicate your thoughts while also maintaining emotional balance?

☐ How do you balance standing up for yourself with showing understanding and patience toward others?

☐ What might happen if you chose to focus on understanding the other person's perspective instead of expressing your own?

☐ How do you think practicing patience in these moments might help protect your sobriety and well-being?

☐ What would it feel like to focus on preserving relationships rather than on addressing every perceived wrong?

☐ When you think about your relationships, what matters most to you in how you connect with others?

☐ What might it feel like to focus on building understanding, even when you feel strongly about something?

☐ How can you honor your feelings while also considering the impact your words have on others?

☐ What helps you find a balance between expressing your thoughts and protecting your relationships?

- How might giving yourself time to reflect change the way you approach difficult situations?
- How do you think practicing patience could help you feel more at ease in your relationships?
- What small steps could you take to focus more on preserving trust and connection with others?

Supporting Long-Term Emotional Growth

- How do you usually feel when you've worked through a challenge without confrontation?
- What are some ways you could take care of yourself when you feel hurt or upset?
- How might learning to pause and reflect before reacting help you feel more in control of your emotions?
- What do you notice about yourself when you handle a difficult moment with kindness and calm?
- How could focusing on your own emotional needs help you feel more balanced in your relationships?
- When you think about growing stronger emotionally, what feels like the first small step you could take?
- How can you remind yourself that you're doing your best, even when things feel frustrating or difficult?

Acknowledging the Current Feelings

- What are you feeling most strongly about this situation right now?
- What's the part of this situation that feels hardest for you to deal with?
- How is this affecting you emotionally in this moment?
- What do you think this situation is bringing up for you that feels so upsetting?
- If you could name the one thing you most want to feel understood about, what would it be?

Exploring Reactions and Responses

- What do you feel like you want to do or say in response to this situation?
- How do you think acting on that impulse might make you feel afterward?
- What usually helps you when you're feeling this way?
- What do you think the other person might feel or understand if you expressed yourself?
- How do you decide when it's best to speak up or to give yourself time to process?

Considering the Bigger Picture

- How does this situation fit into the bigger picture of what matters most to you?

- What would it mean for you to find peace about this, even if it's unresolved?
- When you think about your goals, how does staying calm or reflective help you move toward them?
- How might letting this situation pass benefit you in the long run?
- If this were a smaller moment in your life story, how would you want to handle it?

Encouraging Self-Care and Emotional Balance

- What can you do for yourself right now to feel a little more calm or settled?
- How can you take care of yourself while this situation is still fresh?
- What would help you feel more grounded as you think about this situation?
- How might focusing on your own needs help you manage what's upsetting you?
- What would bring you the most comfort or relief at this moment?

Building Self-Awareness and Letting Go

- How might taking a pause help you feel more in control of this situation?
- What could you notice about your feelings if you gave yourself some space before reacting?

- How could you approach this moment in a way that protects your peace and well-being?
- If you were to let go of some of this upset, how do you think it would feel?
- What's something small you could do to remind yourself that you're doing your best right now?

Fostering Connection and Understanding

- If you could share how you feel with someone you trust, what would you want to say?
- How do you think this situation might look from another perspective?
- What would it mean for you to feel heard and understood about this?
- How can you communicate your feelings in a way that preserves your relationships?
- What do you think could help you feel closer to the people you care about during this time?

Focusing on the Present Feelings and Triggers

- What are you feeling most strongly about this situation right now?
- What's been weighing on your mind the most as this situation unfolded?

□ How do you think holding onto these thoughts or feelings is affecting your peace of mind?

□ How does it feel in your body when you've been thinking about something for a long time?

□ What might help you create a little more mental space from this right now?

Exploring the Link Between Thoughts, Actions, and Sobriety

□ When you're upset like this, how do those feelings impact your commitment to staying sober?

□ What usually happens to your mood and thoughts when you hold onto a situation for too long?

□ How do you think letting these feelings build up could affect your relationships or well-being?

□ How might working through this situation differently help you feel more in control?

□ What would it mean for you to respond in a way that protects your sobriety?

Recognizing Patterns and Developing Insight

□ Have you noticed any patterns in situations where you've felt this way before?

- What typically happens when you act on strong feelings after perseverating for a while?
- How might letting go of some of these thoughts help you avoid a reaction you might regret?
- What do you think fuels your need to hold onto situations like this?
- What might change if you allowed yourself to release these feelings sooner?

Practicing Cognitive Restructuring

- If you stepped back from this situation, how might you see it differently?
- What's another way to think about what happened that feels less upsetting?
- How could this situation look if you focused on your own needs instead of the actions of others?
- What might you say to yourself that could help you move forward without dwelling on it?
- How could reminding yourself of your long-term goals help shift your perspective here?

Building Emotional Regulation Skills

- What are some ways you could calm yourself when you notice your thoughts starting to spiral?

- □ How could you pause and take a step back before reacting to this situation?
- □ What would help you create a sense of balance when you feel overwhelmed like this?
- □ How might taking a break to reflect help you respond in a way that feels better to you?
- □ What could you do to take care of yourself right now instead of focusing on this situation?

Strengthening Self-Commitment and Letting Go

- □ How would letting go of this situation support your goal of staying sober?
- □ What's one small step you could take to let go of some of the tension you're feeling?
- □ How would holding onto this help—or hurt—your long-term goals?
- □ What does it mean to you to protect your peace and your sobriety?
- □ How could you remind yourself that some things are outside of your control?

Encouraging Healthy Communication

- □ How might responding gently or not at all to this situation help avoid unnecessary harm?

- What could you say to someone else that communicates your feelings without escalating things?
- How could you express yourself in a way that prioritizes your peace and well-being?
- What's one way to shift your focus from reacting to reconnecting with those you care about?
- How could stepping back from this situation improve your relationships in the long run?

Linking Actions to Long-Term Sobriety

- When you look back on this moment, how would you want to feel about how you handled it?
- What would it mean for your recovery journey to manage this situation without regret?
- How does working through this challenge help build your confidence in staying sober?
- How could this moment be a chance to practice the skills that protect your sobriety?
- What would it feel like to choose peace for yourself and your recovery right now?

Reflecting on the Situation

- How do you feel now about how things turned out in that situation?

□ What were you hoping to achieve by responding the way you did?

□ Do you feel like your response helped resolve the issue or made it more difficult?

□ How did this situation affect your mood or thoughts afterward?

□ Looking back, what was the hardest part about choosing to let it go?

Exploring Consequences

□ How did your actions impact your relationship with the other person?

□ Did the situation unfold the way you expected it to? Why or why not?

□ What do you think the other person might have felt or thought during this exchange?

□ How did this experience affect your emotional well-being or your recovery journey?

□ What, if anything, might you have lost because of how the situation was handled?

Building Awareness of Patterns

□ Is this similar to any other situations you've experienced in the past? How so?

□ What tends to happen when you hold onto strong feelings like this?

- How often do situations like this leave you feeling satisfied versus regretful?
- What do you notice about your ability to pause before taking action in moments like this?
- How would you describe the thoughts or feelings that make it hard to let go?

Learning from the Experience

- What do you think you could do differently if a similar situation happens again?
- If you were giving advice to someone else in this situation, what would you say?
- What could help you pause and reflect before reacting in a moment of strong emotion?
- How might you remind yourself of your long-term goals in the middle of a tough moment?
- What have you learned about yourself from how this situation turned out?

Encouraging Personal Responsibility

- How much control do you feel you had over your response in that situation?

- How do you think choosing to act differently could change outcomes like this in the future?
- What small steps could you take next time to prevent things from escalating?
- How can you take responsibility for what happened without being too hard on yourself?
- What would it mean to you to take a healthier approach next time?

Reinforcing Commitment to Recovery

- How does managing situations like this connect to your recovery goals?
- How might a different response help you feel stronger in your sobriety?
- What would it feel like to handle situations like this without causing harm or regret?
- How can moments like these become opportunities to grow in your recovery journey?
- What can you do to remind yourself of your commitment to sobriety when you feel upset?

Building Skills for the Future

- What tools or strategies could help you let go of difficult emotions more easily?

☐ How could you practice responding more calmly to situations that upset you?

☐ What are some signs you could look for that you're starting to hold onto something too tightly?

☐ How might practicing relaxation techniques help in moments like this?

☐ What would it take for you to feel comfortable letting go in situations like this?

CHAPTER TWENTY-SIX

Addressing Signs Of Relapse Prompts

Exploring Current Feelings and Behaviors

☐ How have you been feeling emotionally and physically lately?

☐ What have you noticed about your mood or energy levels over the past few days or weeks?

☐ Are there any recent events or situations that have been on your mind more than usual?

☐ How do you feel about the way you've been handling stress lately?

☐ Are you finding it easy or difficult to stay connected to others right now?

Reflecting on Self-Care and Coping

□ How have you been taking care of yourself recently?

□ What activities have been helping you relax or recharge?

□ Are you getting enough sleep, exercise, and nutritious meals?

□ How are you feeling about your ability to cope with challenges right now?

□ What are some things you usually do to keep yourself balanced that you might not be doing lately?

Identifying Early Warning Signs

□ Have you noticed any changes in your thoughts or feelings that seem different from your usual self?

□ Are you finding it harder than usual to manage cravings or intrusive thoughts?

□ Are there any patterns in your thinking or behavior that remind you of times before you relapsed in the past?

□ What do you think might be causing you to feel off-balance lately?

□ Are there any small things that have been bothering you but seem hard to shake?

Encouraging Reflection on Recovery Goals

□ How does how you're feeling now compare to how you felt when you first committed to recovery?

□ What does staying in recovery mean to you right now?

☐ How are your current feelings or behaviors affecting your recovery goals?

☐ What would it feel like to regain a sense of stability and control in your recovery?

☐ What strengths have helped you stay committed to your recovery in the past?

Promoting Action and Self-Efficacy

☐ What do you think you need most right now to feel more grounded?

☐ What small steps could you take today to feel better emotionally or physically?

☐ Are there people in your life you could reach out to for support?

☐ How might revisiting your recovery tools or strategies help you right now?

☐ What would help you feel more confident about handling what you're going through?

Normalizing Struggles and Building Perspective

☐ Is it possible you're going through a rough patch that many people in recovery experience?

☐ What have you learned from past challenges that might help you navigate this moment?

□ How would you remind yourself that ups and downs are a natural part of recovery?

□ How could you show yourself kindness and patience as you work through this?

□ What would it look like to treat yourself with the same care and understanding you'd offer a close friend?

Validation and Normalization

□ It's okay to feel overwhelmed. Recovery isn't about never feeling emotional; it's about learning how to manage those emotions in a healthier way.

□ Many people in recovery face emotional challenges like this. It doesn't mean you're failing—it's just part of the journey.

□ Recognizing that you're struggling is a sign of growth. How does it feel to acknowledge what you're going through?

□ Feeling this way doesn't define your recovery—it's just one moment on a much bigger path.

□ It's natural to feel pulled in different directions emotionally. What matters is how you choose to respond.

□ You're showing courage by facing these feelings. That's an important part of building resilience.

□ What you're feeling right now is something that many of us here can relate to. You're not alone.

□ Recovery is a process, not a straight line. Moments like this are opportunities to learn and grow.

Encouraging Reflection

- [ ] What's one thought or feeling you've been holding onto that feels the heaviest right now?
- [ ] What do you think is underneath the emotions you're feeling? Is there a deeper concern or fear there?
- [ ] How does this moment remind you of past challenges you've faced in recovery?
- [ ] Can you identify a specific trigger for what you're feeling right now?
- [ ] What's one thing you've noticed about your reactions or feelings lately that seems different?
- [ ] Have you noticed any physical signs, like tension or restlessness, that might point to underlying emotions?
- [ ] What's something you wish you could say out loud about what's bothering you?
- [ ] If you could step outside of yourself for a moment, how might you describe what you're experiencing?

Reinforcing Coping Skills

- [ ] When you think about tools you've used in the past, which one feels like it could help right now?
- [ ] What's one small step you could take to reduce the intensity of what you're feeling?

- How might practicing deep breathing or grounding techniques help in this moment?
- Would writing down your thoughts help you organize what you're feeling?
- What could you do right now to give yourself a little relief from this emotional weight?
- How could you use your support network to help navigate what you're feeling?
- What's one thing you could do to take care of yourself emotionally today?
- Have you tried using the ABC tool to break down what's happening and challenge any unhelpful beliefs?

Empowering and Motivating

- What's one thing you've done in the past that shows your strength in handling tough emotions?
- How does your commitment to sobriety give you the power to face this challenge?
- What's one value that helps you stay grounded when things feel overwhelming?
- How could this moment become a stepping stone toward your long-term recovery goals?
- What would success look like for you in handling this situation?
- What's one thing you've learned in recovery that makes you feel capable of handling this?

- How could facing this challenge help you build more confidence in your recovery?
- What's one thing you can do today to remind yourself of your strength and resilience?

Providing Support Without Directing

- What do you think would help you feel more balanced right now?
- Would it help to talk more about what's going on, or focus on solutions?
- How can we as a group support you through this moment?
- What's one area where you feel stuck? Let's explore that together.
- What kind of encouragement or feedback would feel most helpful to you right now?
- How can you use this group as a resource to get through this moment?
- What do you think you need most right now to feel supported?
- What's one way you could remind yourself that you're not alone in this?

Focusing on the Bigger Picture

- When you think about your long-term goals, how does this moment fit into that bigger picture?

- How does staying on your recovery path help you navigate these tough moments?
- What's one thing you want to remember about this experience for the future?
- How could this challenge help you build new skills or insights for your recovery?
- What's one thing about your recovery that you feel proud of, even in this tough moment?
- How does your sobriety protect you from making this moment harder than it needs to be?
- What's one thing you can do to turn this moment into a learning experience?
- What do you want to take from this experience to help you next time something similar happens?

Reminders And Encouragement

- You've handled challenges before, and you can handle this one too.
- This is a moment to lean on your strengths and tools. You've got what it takes.
- Even when it feels hard, you're building skills that make you stronger in recovery.
- You're here, and that shows your commitment to growth and healing.
- This moment doesn't define you. It's what you do with it that matters.

☐ Every step you take to handle this is a step forward in your recovery.

☐ You've already proven how strong and capable you are by choosing this path.

☐ This challenge is just one part of your journey—and you're moving forward.

Identifying Triggers and Early Warning Signs

☐ What are the signs that tell you when you're getting close to the edge of relapse?

☐ When you think about your past experiences, what patterns do you notice before you've relapsed?

☐ What thoughts or feelings tend to come up for you before you feel like you might relapse?

☐ What external situations or stressors seem to make you more vulnerable to relapse?

☐ How can you recognize the first signs of emotional or mental struggle that might lead to relapse?

☐ What are the small decisions you could make early on to prevent things from escalating?

☐ How can you tell when you're starting to feel overwhelmed, and what would you do differently if you noticed it sooner?

Developing Coping Strategies

□ What is one thing you can do in the moment to calm yourself when you're feeling tempted to relapse?

□ What coping mechanisms have worked for you in the past when you've felt close to relapse?

□ If you could write down a few steps to take when you're feeling triggered, what would they look like?

□ What is a self-care practice that you can turn to when you sense a relapse might be near?

□ How might distracting yourself or changing your environment help you in these moments?

□ What activities or hobbies could help redirect your focus when you feel the urge to use?

□ How can you reframe your thoughts in moments when you're feeling low or stressed, to avoid slipping back into old habits?

Building a Support System

□ Who are the people in your life you can call when you sense you're nearing a relapse, and what can you ask them to do for you?

□ What kind of support or encouragement would help you the most when you're at risk of relapse?

□ How can you reach out for support in a way that feels comfortable to you during these times?

□ What would you need from this group or your support network to help you stay on track when things get tough?

- How can you remind yourself that you don't have to face this on your own?
- Is there a person or a community you could check in with before things get too hard?

Creating a Plan of Action

- What's a simple, clear plan you can put into action when you feel a relapse might be near?
- What are some immediate actions you could take to help you shift your focus away from using?
- How could you break down a relapse situation into small steps, making it easier to navigate?
- What's a small goal you can set for yourself today, to build momentum for avoiding relapse in the future?
- What might be your first step when you realize you're feeling at risk for relapse?
- How can you remind yourself of the reasons you chose recovery in moments of temptation?
- What's one thing you can do each day to strengthen your resolve and prepare for tough moments ahead?
- When you feel like you might relapse, what's the one thought you can repeat to yourself to stay grounded?

Strengthening Motivation for Sobriety

- What motivates you to stay sober, even when you're struggling? How can you reconnect with that motivation in tough times?
- How would you feel if you successfully avoided relapse and continued your progress in recovery?
- When you picture your life a year from now, how does staying sober contribute to that vision?
- What positive changes have you seen in your life since you began recovery that you want to keep moving forward with?
- What is one thing you'd like to achieve in your life if you continue to stay sober? How can you use that as motivation?
- What does sobriety give you that you value deeply, and how can that help you when things feel hard?
- How can focusing on your long-term goals help you in the moments when you're tempted to relapse?

Reflecting on the Past and Learning from Mistakes

- What did you learn from previous relapses that you could apply to your plan for today?
- How did you feel after a relapse, and how can that feeling remind you of why you want to stay sober?
- What was it about those previous moments of relapse that you wish you could have done differently?
- If you could go back and change one thing during your last relapse, what would it be?

□ How can you use your past experiences to prepare yourself better for future challenges?

□ What has your journey of recovery taught you about what helps you most when life feels unmanageable?

Evaluating Success and Adjusting the Plan

□ How will you know if your plan is working, and what signs will you look for to make sure you're on track?

□ What could you adjust in your plan if you find that certain triggers keep coming up?

□ What would success in preventing relapse look like to you in this situation, and how can you celebrate that success?

□ How can you continue to adjust and improve your plan as you learn more about yourself and your recovery needs?

□ What can you learn from each situation when you make it through a difficult moment without relapsing?

□ What steps can you take to ensure your plan remains strong and relevant as you continue your recovery journey?

Reaffirming Commitment to Sobriety

□ How will you remind yourself of your commitment to sobriety every day, especially during challenging times?

☐ What personal strengths can you draw upon in these moments to help you avoid relapse?

☐ What will you do to reaffirm your commitment to your recovery and remind yourself that you are worth it?

☐ What does sobriety allow you to experience in your life that you wouldn't want to lose?

☐ How do you want to feel at the end of each day, knowing you made choices that support your long-term goals?

☐ What does your recovery mean to you, and how can that meaning help you stay focused on your goals?

CHAPTER TWENTY-SEVEN

Putting A Crisis Plan In Place Prompts

Identifying Support Needs in a Crisis

☐ When you think about what you might need in a moment when relapse feels imminent, what types of support come to mind?

☐ Who in your life would you feel comfortable reaching out to for help when you're struggling with the urge to relapse?

☐ What would you need from your support network to feel heard and supported during tough times?

☐ In those intense moments when you're at risk of relapse, how could others best support you without making you feel judged?

☐ What specific kind of emotional support would be most helpful to you when you're feeling overwhelmed and close to relapsing?

□ Are there certain people or resources you would want to reach out to immediately if you were feeling like you might relapse?

□ How would you prefer someone offer encouragement during a difficult moment, so it feels more motivating than overwhelming?

□ If you were to ask for support in a difficult situation, what would you need from that person to feel like you're not alone in the moment?

Creating Immediate Action Plans and Tools

□ What could you do in the first few minutes when you sense relapse is close? How can you prepare for that moment?

□ What kind of action plan would help you shift your focus in the moments when you feel an urge to use?

□ Is there a specific coping strategy or activity that has worked in the past that you could turn to immediately in those moments?

□ What tools could you have at hand—such as breathing techniques, self-talk, or other strategies—that could help you gain control when the urge to relapse arises?

□ How could a phone call, text, or message from someone you trust help you refocus when you're at risk of relapse?

□ What type of immediate distractions or activities could you incorporate into your plan to help break the thought cycle of relapse?

□ What specific self-care practices might help you feel better in the moment, so you're less vulnerable to the urge to drink?

☐ If you could write down three things to do immediately when you feel tempted to relapse, what would they be?

Identifying Information Needs

☐ What kind of information would you want available to you in a moment when you're at risk of relapse?

☐ If you could have a list of reminders or key points to look at during difficult moments, what would they say?

☐ What would help you remember why you've chosen sobriety and how to stay focused in a moment of vulnerability?

☐ If you had a quick reference guide or tool, what type of information would you like it to include to keep you grounded during a crisis?

☐ Would having a list of past successes or reasons for staying sober help you in those moments? What would you include on that list?

☐ Is there a specific affirmation or mantra that you would want to repeat to yourself when the pressure feels overwhelming?

☐ If you had a mental checklist of things to do when relapse feels near, what would be the top few items on that list?

☐ How could tracking your progress and remembering how far you've come help you stay motivated in the face of temptation?

Exploring External Support Resources

- What types of professional support would you feel comfortable reaching out to when you're feeling at risk of relapse?
- Would attending a meeting or therapy session provide support in moments of crisis? If so, what would make that most helpful?
- Is there a specific hotline, app, or online resource that you could use to get support or guidance during those moments?
- How would it help to have a backup plan, like a list of numbers to call or people to contact, when you're feeling triggered?
- What external tools or strategies (like journaling or mindfulness apps) would be useful to you when you're facing intense cravings or emotions?
- Would reaching out to someone outside of your immediate circle, like a support group or mentor, be something you could turn to when needed?
- What kind of professional support—like a counselor, therapist, or recovery coach—could help guide you during tough moments?

Reflecting on Past Experiences

- Looking back, what types of support have worked for you in the past when you've felt at risk of relapse?
- What actions or tools have helped you before when you've been in a similar position? How can you use that experience to guide you now?
- When you've successfully avoided relapse in the past, what did you do differently that helped you stay on track?

◻ What advice would you give yourself if you were facing a moment of crisis in the future based on what you've learned from your past experiences?
◻ How did you feel when you made it through a tough moment without relapsing? What did you learn from that experience that you could apply in the future?

CHAPTER TWENTY-EIGHT

Freeze-Frame Scenarios ™

How To Use Freeze-Frame Scenarios:

Your best friend, Alex, has been on a journey of recovery—one you've been part of every step of the way. Over time, you've come to know Alex's struggles, strengths, and fears. You've celebrated milestones together and supported each other through tough conversations. Alex trusts you to be present in the moments that matter most.

You have agreed to be Alex's Recovery Ally—a trusted support during difficult moments. Alex knows you'll be honest, compassionate, and steady when things feel uncertain.

The following moments capture real challenges Alex is facing. As you respond, think about the person you know—not just someone struggling with recovery, but a friend with history, depth, and complexity.

Each scenario unfolds as if you are watching it play out on a private stage. You see Alex moving through a challenge, caught in a decision point. Then—**freeze-frame.** The movement stops. The background fades. The noise disappears. Alex turns to face you directly, waiting.

Alex cannot respond or react in this moment. This is your chance to speak freely—to offer the guidance and care you know your best friend needs.

Your answers might change over time. You may approach these situations differently a month from now, or even tomorrow. Consider revisiting them. Growth isn't a straight line, and neither is perspective.

And here's the real insight: The way you comfort and guide Alex is exactly how you deserve to treat yourself. These prompts can also help you preplan how you might respond when similar situations impact you.

Recovery brings unpredictable challenges—grief, disappointment, stress, and moments of overwhelming temptation. Having a crisis plan in place can make all the difference. Each of these scenarios offers an opportunity to think ahead, preparing strategies for staying on track when faced with life's toughest moments.

CHAPTER TWENTY-NINE

Standing at the Doorway of the Past

Alex wasn't sure about coming in the first place. The invitation wasn't to just any bar—it was *the* bar. The one where the worst nights happened, and the best nights turned into regrets.

But tonight, it's someone's birthday. People from work will be there. It felt harmless enough at first. The door swings open. Music pulses through the space. Glasses clink. The thick scent of alcohol wraps around Alex before even stepping inside.

Feet planted at the threshold, Alex suddenly feels rooted to the spot.

Freeze-frame.
Alex turns to you, waiting.

☐ How do you respond?

☐ What could you say to help Alex stay grounded and remember why this choice matters?

☐ What options might help Alex feel more comfortable—or leave without shame?

CHAPTER THIRTY

An Honest Mistake with Big Implications

A familiar knock at the door.

Alex grins before even opening it. This friend is someone who *should* know about the recovery journey. Alex had mentioned it before—maybe not in deep conversations, but enough times that it should be understood.

They hug, laughter spilling into the space. The easy kind of reunion that makes it feel like no time has passed. The friend sets a bag down, pulling out a bottle of wine.

"I grabbed this on the way over—figured we could celebrate catching up!"

There's no pressure, no *"just one won't hurt."* It's an honest misunderstanding. The friend doesn't seem to realize the weight of what they've done.

Alex hesitates, glancing at you.

Freeze-frame.

Alex turns to you, waiting.

☐ If Alex looked to you for guidance, what would you say?

☐ How could you help Alex navigate this moment without making it awkward?

☐ What's a way for Alex to set a boundary while staying true to this path?

CHAPTER THIRTY-ONE

Unwinding Without the Old Habit

The apartment is dim, save for the blue glow of a TV. Alex slouches deep into the couch, rubbing temples, jaw tight. It's been a brutal day. The kind where everything small became a fight—emails, conversations, people who didn't even *mean* to be annoying but still were.

A deep sigh. Shoes kicked off. Fingers drumming against the armrest.

"I don't know how people unwind without drinking. I just want to shut it all off for a while."

Freeze-frame.

Alex turns to you, waiting.

☐ How would you respond in a way that supports Alex without judgment?

☐ What healthier ways to unwind could you explore together?

☐ How could you help Alex reconnect with past successes in managing stress differently?

CHAPTER THIRTY-TWO

The Late-Night Call for Escape

The phone rings late. Too late for casual conversation.

You answer to silence. Then, a breath—unsteady, heavy.

"I don't know what to do with this feeling."

Alex's voice is thick, raw.

"I just need to shut it off. Just for a little while."

There's a pause. A small, shaky laugh that doesn't sound like laughter at all.

"I mean, what's the harm? Just tonight, right?"

A sound on the other end. A bottle cap twisting? The rustle of something being opened? The barely-there clink of glass against a counter?

Freeze-frame.

Alex is waiting.

☐ How would you respond over the phone to offer comfort, even from a distance?

☐ What healthier coping strategies could you suggest?

☐ What could you ask to help Alex process these emotions rather than numb them?

CHAPTER THIRTY-THREE

Pressure to Celebrate the "Right" Way

The scent of grilled food and something sweet—maybe caramelized onions, maybe a dessert—drifts through the air.

Laughter ripples through the restaurant, silverware clinking, glasses raised in toasts.

Alex sits at the center of it all, the promotion—the long hours, the extra work, all of it finally paying off. People cheer, pat Alex on the back, and offer congratulations.

"Come on, Alex! This calls for a real toast!"

A cocktail slides across the table. A beer. Something bright and fizzy.

Alex's fingers curl against the tabletop. A slight shift in weight, like indecision, has a physical pull.

Freeze-frame.

Alex is waiting.

☐ How would you help Alex enjoy the celebration without feeling the pull of old habits?

☐ What are some alternative ways Alex could make the night feel just as special?

CHAPTER THIRTY-FOUR

The Weight Of Self-Doubt

A desk scattered with papers. An unfinished email glowing on the screen. Alex sits motionless, staring at it. The cursor blinks, waiting.

"I'm never going to make it."

The voice is flat. Not dramatic, not seeking reassurance—just stating a fact.

"I don't know why I even try."

Freeze-frame.

Alex is waiting.

☐ If Alex said this aloud to you, how would you respond?

☐ What could you say to help Alex see progress instead of setbacks?

☐ How could you encourage self-compassion instead of self-criticism?

CHAPTER THIRTY-FIVE

A Slip, Not a Fall

Morning light spills across the coffee table, illuminating the half-empty glass. The bottle—mostly drained—sits just beside it. A jacket tossed carelessly over the couch. Shoes left haphazardly near the door. The stale scent of alcohol lingers in the air.

Alex sits in the middle of it all, hands pressed together, staring down.

"I let everyone down. I don't know if I can keep going."

Freeze-frame.

Alex is waiting.

☐ How would you respond to remind Alex that one moment doesn't define the journey?

☐ What could you say to help shift the focus from shame to learning and growth?

□ What small steps might help Alex regain confidence and move forward?

CHAPTER THIRTY-SIX

An Old Temptation in the Closet

The dull ache has been building all day. A familiar, unwelcome presence. By evening, Alex is sitting stiffly, one hand gripping a sore shoulder, the other pressed into an aching lower back.

The usual strategies aren't working today. Stretching didn't help. Deep breathing did nothing. Ice only numbed it for a moment. A sharp pang shoots through Alex's ribs, forcing a long, shaky breath.

The thought surfaces before it can be stopped.

Alex walks to the bedroom closet, hesitates, then pulls open the top drawer. Beneath some old paperwork and tangled cords, fingers brush against something cool and solid.

It's been there for a while. Kept *just in case.*

Alex stares at it, shoulders tense.

Freeze-frame.

Alex turns to you, waiting.

□ What could be said to acknowledge the difficulty of this moment with empathy?

□ What alternative pain management strategies might help right now?

□ What words of encouragement could reinforce the commitment to staying on track?

CHAPTER THIRTY-SEVEN

The Return Of Cravings After Four Months

Four months in.

Alex thought this part was in the rearview mirror. The cravings had been strong in the beginning, but for a while now, they had faded—like background noise barely worth noticing.

But tonight, out of nowhere, the urge slams in like a wave.

Hands feel unsteady. The air is thick, hard to pull into the lungs. The mind sharpens in a way Alex didn't expect, pinpoint-focused on using. It's a gnawing hunger, nothing like the first few weeks. This is different.

"I thought I was past this."

Frustration creeps in. It wasn't supposed to feel this strong again.

Freeze-frame.

Alex turns to you, waiting.

☐ How could this experience be reframed to ease frustration?

☐ What strategies might make it easier to ride out the craving?

☐ How might this moment be used to reconnect Alex to those original personal reasons for change?

CHAPTER THIRTY-EIGHT

The Past Looks Better Than It Was

The photo stops Alex mid-scroll.

A group of friends, arms slung around each other, faces glowing with laughter. Bottles raised in a toast, catching the dim bar light.

Alex pauses, eyes lingering on the image. The longer they stare, the more the picture seems to move—like a memory slipping into the present. The music, the buzz of conversation, the warmth of a drink in hand.

For a moment, everything else fades.

"I miss that."

The thought lands softly, unspoken.

Freeze-frame.

Alex turns to you, waiting.

□ What could be said to help balance nostalgia with reality?

□ How might it be helpful to revisit Alex's original reasons for quitting?

□ What new ways of creating meaningful moments could be explored?

CHAPTER THIRTY-NINE

A Weekend Without the Old Routine

Friday night.

Alex stands in the kitchen, staring at the fridge. The room is too quiet. The whole apartment is too quiet.

The weekend drinking always started around now. That first pour, that first sip—like flipping a switch, shifting into something looser, something easier. The workweek's weight lifted.

Alex closes the fridge without taking anything out and turns away. Paces the length of the room. Checks the phone. Sits on the couch. Stands up again.

The hours ahead stretch out, hollow and unfamiliar.

"What do I even do with this time?"

Freeze-frame.

Alex turns to you, waiting.

☐ How could progress in breaking old patterns be recognized?
☐ What new routines or activities might help fill this space?
☐ What could make the adjustment to weekends without alcohol feel more natural?

CHAPTER FORTY

Feeling Left Behind in Friendships

Alex is scrolling mindlessly, letting post after post blur past.

Then—one stops the momentum.

An old friend. A rooftop bar. A caption filled with inside jokes.

The feeling is immediate. That old tug. It's not the drinking itself—it's the space Alex no longer occupies. The easy laughter, the sense of belonging, the way the night used to unfold without a second thought.

Fingers hover over the screen. For a moment, Alex considers sending a message.

"What if I just went?"

Not to drink. Just to be there. Just to feel part of it again.

Freeze-frame.

Alex turns to you, waiting.

□ How could these emotions be processed without judgment?

□ What alternative ways of maintaining social connection could be explored?

□ What steps might help reinforce Alex's commitment to a new path?

CHAPTER FORTY-ONE

A Familiar Smell Outside the Bar

The laughter spills out from the bar doors before Alex even sees the sign.

It's the kind of night that used to be automatic—music, good company, the easy pleasure of melting into a crowd.

A group stands near the entrance, talking between drags of cigarettes. The sharp, familiar scent drifts toward Alex, triggering something unspoken.

A memory stirs.

For a second, Alex just stands there, watching.

"I could go inside. Just for old times' sake."

A step forward.

Freeze-frame.

Alex turns to you, waiting.

☐ What could be said to help Alex pause and think before acting?

☐ How might this moment be used to reconnect Alex to those original personal reasons for change?

☐ What alternatives could offer the same sense of enjoyment without drinking?

CHAPTER FORTY-TWO

A Family Gathering Without Wine

The rich scent of home-cooked food lingers in the air. The dining room glows under the soft light of a chandelier. Silverware clinks against plates, conversation weaves through the space.

Alex knew this was coming. Family gatherings always go the same way—good food, long conversations, and wine poured freely.

A relative reaches for a bottle of wine, pausing before filling Alex's glass.

"Oh, wait—do you still drink?"

It's not mocking. Not pushing. Just an honest question, laced with a hint of awkwardness. The glass is placed on the table near Alex's plate, an unspoken offering.

Eyes flick up, waiting for the answer.

Freeze-frame.

Alex turns to you, waiting.

□ How could a confident and comfortable response be prepared in advance?

□ What could help strengthen Alex's sense of personal choice in this moment?

□ How might this gathering be fully enjoyed without drinking?

CHAPTER FORTY-THREE

A Familiar Invitation, A Risky Choice

Alex turns the corner and nearly bumps into an old friend.

"Alex! No way! It's been forever—come grab a drink with me!"

The excitement in the friend's voice is genuine. The invitation isn't meant to tempt or pressure—just a familiar way to reconnect.

Alex hesitates. The old rhythm of meeting up over drinks feels automatic. Turning it down seems like rejecting the friendship, but accepting feels like stepping onto dangerous ground.

"Yeah... maybe."

The words slip out before Alex can decide what to do.

Freeze-frame.

Alex turns to you, waiting.

□ How could this moment be navigated in a way that protects recovery while keeping the friendship intact?

□ What alternatives to drinking could be suggested for catching up?

□ How might Alex focus on personal well-being instead of people-pleasing?

CHAPTER FORTY-FOUR

Triggered by a TV Scene

A soft glow flickers from the television as Alex lounges on the couch, half-watching a show.

Onscreen, two characters laugh as they pour drinks, glasses clinking in celebration. It's such a simple, everyday moment.

Without thinking, Alex swallows hard.

The thought is immediate, intrusive.

"That looks good right now."

A familiar itch creeps in, the kind that makes it hard to focus on anything else.

Freeze-frame.

Alex turns to you, waiting.

☐ How could this moment be reframed to shift perspective?

☐ What action could help break the cycle of temptation?

CHAPTER FORTY-FIVE

The Argument That Won't Let Go

The argument was loud, messy—one of those fights that lingers long after the shouting stops.

Alex slams the bedroom door, breath coming fast and shallow. Shoulders tight, jaw clenched, muscles coiled as if still ready to argue. The words still ring in the ears, playing on a loop.

Everything feels wrong. Too sharp, too loud, too much.

The thought surfaces before it can be stopped.

Something to dull this feeling. Something to smooth out the jagged edges.

Eyes flick toward the kitchen. A familiar pull rises in the chest.

Freeze-frame.

Alex turns to you, waiting.

◻ What could be done to manage these emotions without turning to alcohol?

◻ What healthier ways could be used to cool down and reflect?

◻ How might this moment be used to recognize that drinking won't resolve the conflict?

CHAPTER FORTY-SIX

Left Out and Looking Back

Alex watches from the phone screen as a group of friends laugh together, drinks in hand, snapping selfies.

The pictures blur at the edges, stomach tightening with something hard to name. It's not just about *this* night.

It's the memory of standing at the edge of a group in middle school, trying to laugh at the right moments. It's hearing inside jokes that don't make sense anymore. It's realizing, in real time, how life moves on without asking permission.

The feeling lands like a weight in the chest.

"Maybe I don't belong anywhere anymore."

Freeze-frame.

Alex turns to you, waiting.

▢ How could this moment be reframed to ease feelings of exclusion?

▢ What steps could be taken to build connections that support recovery?

▢ How might this moment reinforce the reasons behind choosing this path?

CHAPTER FORTY-SEVEN

Grief, Overwhelm, and the Urge to Escape

The words hit hard.

The phone call is over, but the weight of the bad news lingers, heavy and suffocating.

Alex presses fingers to temples, breathing unsteady.

"I don't know how to deal with this."

The thought is almost instinctual. Escape. Numb it out. Make it stop.

Freeze-frame.

Alex turns to you, waiting.

☐ How could healthier coping strategies be encouraged in this moment?

◻ What reminders might help validate emotions without avoiding them?

◻ What self-care actions could be taken instead of reaching for a drink?

CHAPTER FORTY-EIGHT

Doubting The Right To Recovery

Alex stares at the ceiling, unable to push the memories away.

Not the good ones. The bad ones. The nights that ended in slurred words and slammed doors. The people who were hurt—some who forgave, some who never will.

The heaviness in the chest turns sharp, breath catching in the throat.

"Maybe I don't deserve to be sober."

The thought feels too big. Too permanent. If all the damage is already done, what's the point of trying to change?

Freeze-frame.

Alex turns to you, waiting.

☐ What could be said to encourage self-compassion?

☐ How might this moment be used to shift from self-punishment to growth?

☐ What steps could be taken to move forward instead of dwelling in regret?

CHAPTER FORTY-NINE

Restless Nights and Racing Thoughts

Alex stares at the ceiling, exhausted but restless.

Every time the eyes close, thoughts surge in—unfinished tasks, old regrets, worries that seemed small in daylight but feel enormous now.

It's been almost an hour. Sleep won't come.

"I need to relax somehow."

Freeze-frame.

Alex turns to you, waiting.

☐ What relaxation techniques might help in this moment?

☐ How could this be reframed to recognize that alcohol wouldn't solve the real problem?

☐ What healthier nighttime routines could be established?

CHAPTER FIFTY

Misreading The Body's Needs

Alex feels the dizziness first.

The day was busy—too busy. There hadn't been time to eat, and now, lightheaded and unfocused, the craving kicks in.

Not for food. Not for water. But for a drink.

The automatic response is unsettling.

Freeze-frame.

Alex turns to you, waiting.

☐ How could this moment be used to recognize what the body actually needs?

☐ What small, immediate steps might help restore balance?

☐ How could new habits be built to prevent hunger and thirst from turning into cravings?

CHAPTER FIFTY-ONE

The Routine That No Longer Fits

Alex leans against the fence, heart still pounding from the run.

For years, finishing a workout came with a reward—one cold drink, then maybe another.

Now, muscles ache, sweat drips, and the craving kicks in hard.

"That would hit the spot right now."

Freeze-frame.

Alex turns to you, waiting.

☐ What other rewarding post-workout habits might be helpful?

☐ How could this craving be recognized as temporary?

☐ What could be done in this moment to feel accomplished without alcohol?

CHAPTER FIFTY-TWO

A Slip Toward Old Thinking

Alex hasn't had a drink in months, but the thought comes casually, out of nowhere.

"Maybe I can handle just one now."

It's small, subtle—an idea that tugs at the edges of logic.

Freeze-frame.

Alex turns to you, waiting.

□ How could this thought be challenged in a way that encourages reflection?

□ What past experiences might help counter this thinking?

□ What steps could help Alex stay grounded in the original commitment?

CHAPTER FIFTY-THREE

Memories Of An Ex And The Pull Of The Past

Alex's phone vibrates. A notification.

The name sends a jolt through the chest—an ex, someone from the past.

The photo attached to the post makes it worse: drinks in hand, grinning. A snapshot from a different time.

Nostalgia crashes in hard.

Freeze-frame.

Alex turns to you, waiting.

□ How could detachment from this memory be encouraged?

□ What reminders might help separate nostalgia from reality?

☐ How might this moment be used to refocus on a future that aligns with recovery?

CHAPTER FIFTY-FOUR

A Fading Will

The apartment is quiet, too quiet. The kind of silence that feels heavier than noise. Alex sits on the couch, scrolling aimlessly.

A half-written text to a recovery friend lingers on the screen—typed, erased, retyped, and then abandoned. The last meeting?

Missed.

The journal?

Left untouched.

That book about recovery, the one that once felt so inspiring, sits on the table, collecting dust.

"I don't even know why I'm doing this anymore."

The thought isn't loud, but it's persistent. The excitement, the relief of early recovery—that feeling of *finally getting somewhere*—it's all dulled. Lately, everything feels like going through the motions.

Skipping the next meeting wouldn't matter.

Ignoring the check-in wouldn't change anything.

Just one day of isolating—what difference does it make?

Freeze-frame.

Alex turns to you, waiting.

☐ What are the warning signs in this moment that need to be addressed?

☐ How could Alex reconnect with the reasons recovery mattered in the first place?

☐ What small action could shift the momentum before this feeling deepens?

CHAPTER FIFTY-FIVE

Grudge

The text sits unread.

Alex knows what it says without opening it.

It's from someone who was there during the worst moments. Someone who *saw* everything. Someone who, even now, even after all the work, still doesn't believe Alex can change.

"People don't really change."

Those were the last words they said before cutting contact.

Now, months later, they've reached out—but not with an apology. Not with a second chance. Just something casual, like everything that happened before doesn't exist.

Alex's jaw tightens, pulse ticking in the throat.

The unfairness of it sticks like a splinter. The work, the effort, the constant fight to be better—and yet, some people still refuse to see it.

The urge isn't to drink.

It's to *lash out*.

To demand to be seen.

To prove something.

To let this anger *burn through* the frustration.

Freeze-frame.

Alex turns to you, waiting.

☐ How could this resentment be processed in a way that supports healing instead of harm?

☐ What reminders might help Alex accept that not everyone will acknowledge the work being done?

☐ What action could help shift the focus back to self-growth rather than seeking external validation?

CHAPTER FIFTY-SIX

The Final Chapter

THE BRAIN, THE PATTERNS, AND THE WAY OUT

Alcohol, through the slow process of addiction, rewires the brain to respond to chemical inputs with chemical outputs. Thoughts go in... emotions go in... through the rewired circuits. That's learning through repetition.

The synapses of the brain, in their rewiring, become watchful, expectant, anticipatory. This isn't just theory—it's neuroscience. Alcohol addiction physically alters neurotransmitter systems, including GABA and glutamate, as the brain fights to maintain homeostasis. The body reacts to alcohol's depressive effects with stimulants, and those stimulants? They don't just vanish. They interrupt sleep, amplify anxiety, and leave the body scrambling to find balance.

Dehydration weakens the body. Sleep is meant to heal, but when the body is still working to clear toxins and counteract stimulation, it can't. The person wakes up unrested. Stimulants, unchecked, express themselves as anxiety. Emotions flare. The body is exhausted yet overstimulated, stuck in a rhythm it never chose but can't seem to escape.

This cycle isn't just frustrating—it's dangerous. Day in, day out. The brain is watching, learning, deepening the pattern. That's how addiction carves its path: through practice, through repetition.

By the time addiction has taken hold, behavioral and thought patterns are no longer choices—they're habits. They feel automatic. The body is exhausted, tense, desperate to recover. But it never does, sliding down the slippery chutes of addiction's spiral.

This isn't just about behavior; it's about brain function. The same neural processes that help us master a skill—driving, typing, playing an instrument—lock addiction into place. It's not just habit. It's hardwiring. And that's where the real risk comes in.

The addicted brain no longer needs permission. It operates on autopilot, watching for familiar stressors—anxiety, fatigue, emotional turmoil. These signals, once tied to drinking, are familiar. The neural pathways light up, preparing the brain to respond the way it was trained to. And when that happens? Choice becomes a far-off concept.

There's something else to know. The kindling effect. It's real, and it's brutal. Repeated cycles of relapse and recovery make withdrawal worse each time. The symptoms get stronger, the risks more serious. Alcohol changes the brain, and at a certain point, some of those changes become permanent.

This isn't just a possibility—it's documented. Studies confirm that repeated withdrawal intensifies symptoms and increases the likelihood of lasting damage. The point of no return is real, and many people don't realize they're approaching it until it's too late.

Earlier, I shared the story of someone who reached that point. He went in and out of rehab, unable to hold onto recovery. Then, one day, he was gone. I tried to make sense of it. Was it his dopamine levels, eroded beyond repair? Was it despair that swallowed him whole?

Now, with a deeper understanding of how the addicted brain functions, I see what likely happened. His addiction wasn't just a pattern. It was automatic. His brain, rewired and hypervigilant, had trained itself to relapse. And at some point, the ability to resist may have disappeared altogether.

This book isn't about fear. It's about understanding. It's about equipping people with knowledge and tools to navigate recovery successfully. Lifelong sobriety is possible, but it takes strategy, support, and rewiring the brain for something new.

The Alcohol Recovery Ally is here for that reason. To make information accessible, to ensure it's understandable, to give people a fighting chance at a different future. And not just in the early days of recovery, but in every stage that follows.

I mentioned earning my certification to facilitate recovery groups. Facilitators ask more questions than they answer. That's because learning happens through discovery. In writing this book, I found myself engaging in that same process—asking the questions, uncovering answers, and organizing knowledge in ways I had not seen compiled before.

Yet, I hesitated to start a group. I questioned my role—an educator, not a therapist. But if this book allows me to serve as a different kind of Recovery Ally—the author of a book that provides ongoing support, accessible whenever a reader needs it—then I am more than happy to call my readers my first group. Through this content, they will explore their own questions, uncover their own answers, and discover what recovery means for them. The research is undeniable—50 to 70 percent of individuals recovering from alcohol addiction relapse at least once. If any single program guaranteed lifelong sobriety, those numbers wouldn't be so staggering. Clearly, we need more. That's why The Alcohol Recovery Ally was born.

Because information saves lives. Because understanding dismantles fear. And because, as a friend once said to me, "I hope you help someone."

CHAPTER FIFTY-SEVEN

References

Alcohol Help. (2019). The three stages of relapse. Retrieved from
https://www.alcoholhelp.com/blog/three-stages-relapse/

American Addiction Centers. (2025). Alcohol withdrawal symptoms, detox, timeline, and treatment.https://americanadd
ictioncenters.org/alcohol/withdrawal-detox

American Psychological Association. (n.d.). Understanding alcohol use disorders and their treatment. Retrieved
from https://www.apa.org/topics/substance-use-abuse-ad
diction/alcohol-disorders

American Psychological Association. (n.d.). What is cognitive behavioral therapy? Retrieved from https://www.apa.org/pts
d-guideline/patients-and-families/cognitive-behavioral

Beck, J. S. (2011). Cognitive behavior therapy: Basics and beyond
(2nd ed.). The Guilford Press.

Berking, M., Margraf, M., Ebert, D., Wupperman, P., Hofmann, S. G., & Junghanns, K. (2011). Deficits in emotion-regulation skills predict alcohol use during and after cognitive-behavioral therapy for alcohol dependence. *Journal of Consulting and Clinical Psychology, 79*(3), 307–318. https://doi.org/1 0.1037/a0023421

Berridge, K. C., & Robinson, T. E. (2016). Liking, wanting, and the incentive-sensitization theory of addiction. The American Psychologist, 71(8), 670–679. https://doi.org/10.1037/am p0000059

Brown, B. (2012). Daring greatly: How the courage to be vulnerable transforms the way we live, love, parent, and lead.Goth am Books.

Carroll, K. M., & Onken, L. S. (2005). Behavioral therapies for drug abuse. The American Journal of Psychiatry, 162(8), 1452–1460. https://doi.org/10.1176/appi.ajp.162.8.1452

Carr, A. (2015). Allen Carr's quit drinking without willpower: Be a happy non-drinker. Arcturus Publishing Limited.

Ellis, A. (2006). How to stubbornly refuse to make yourself miserable about anything—Yes, anything! Citadel Press.

Flores, P. J. (2004). Addiction as an attachment disorder. Jason Aronson.

Hall, W. (2017). Alcohol explained. Independently published.

Harris, R. (2009). ACT made simple: An easy-to-read primer on acceptance and commitment therapy. New Harbinger Publications.

Hayes, S. C., Strosahl, K. D., & Wilson, K. G. (2016). Acceptance and commitment therapy: The process and practice of mindful change (2nd ed.). The Guilford Press.

Hogan, S. (2022). Dialectical behavior therapy for addiction: The easy self-help guide - Simple steps to conquering addictions to porn - eating disorders - substance abuse - alcohol and drugs - online gambling.

Kelly, J. F., & Greene, M. C. (2014). Where there's a will there's a way: A longitudinal study of financial recovery from addiction. Addiction, 109(3), 472–481. https://doi.org/10.1111/add.12469

Koob, G. F., & Volkow, N. D. (2016). Neurobiology of addiction: A neurocircuitry analysis. The Lancet Psychiatry, 3(8), 760–773. https://doi.org/10.1016/S2215-0366(16)00104-8

Linehan, M. M. (2014). DBT skills training manual (2nd ed.). The Guilford Press.

Marlatt, G. A., & Donovan, D. M. (Eds.). (2005). Relapse prevention: Maintenance strategies in the treatment of addictive behaviors (2nd ed.). The Guilford Press.

McHugh, R. K., Hearon, B. A., & Otto, M. W. (2010). Cognitive-behavioral therapy for substance use disorders.Psychiatric Clinics of North America, 33(3), 511–525.
https://doi.org/10.1016/j.psc.2010.04.012

McKay, D. (2022). DBT for dummies. For Dummies.

McKay, M. (2020). DBT made simple: A step-by-step guide to dialectical behavior therapy (2nd ed.). New Harbinger Publications.

McKelvey, J., Thrul, J., & Ramo, D. E. (2022). Smoking as an outcome moderator in the treatment of alcohol use disorder: Effects on coping skills, self-efficacy, and alcohol use. *Alcohol and Alcoholism, 57*(6), 664–671. https://doi.org/10.1093/alcalc/agac039

Miller, W. R., & Rollnick, S. (2013). Motivational interviewing: Helping people change (3rd ed.). The Guilford Press.

Moos, R. H. (2007). Theory-based processes that promote the remission of substance use disorders. Clinical Psychology Review, 27(5), 537–551. https://doi.org/10.1016/j.cpr.2006.12.006

Moos, R. H., & Moos, B. S. (2006). Rates and predictors of relapse after natural and treated remission from alcohol use disorders. Addiction, 101(2), 212–222. https://doi.org/10.1111/j.1360-0443.2006.01310.x

National Institute on Alcohol Abuse and Alcoholism. (2025, January). *Neuroscience: The brain in addiction and recovery.* Retrieved from https://www.niaaa.nih.gov/health-professionals-communities/core-resource-on-alcohol/neuroscience-brain-addiction-and-recovery.

National Institute on Alcohol Abuse and Alcoholism. (n.d.). Treatment for alcohol problems: Finding and getting help.Retrieved from https://www.niaaa.nih.gov/publications/brochures-and-fact-sheets/treatment-alcohol-problems-finding-and-getting-help

National Institute on Drug Abuse. (2020). Drugs, brains, and behavior: The science of addiction. Retrieved from https://nida.nih.gov/publications/drugs-brains-behavior-science-addiction

Nowinski, J. (2015). If you work it, it works!: The science behind 12-step recovery. Hazelden Publishing.

OpenAI. (2025). ChatGPT (Feb 6 version) [Large language model]. https://openai.com

Peele, S. (2016). Recover! Stop thinking like an addict and reclaim your life with the PERFECT program. Da Capo Press.

Schweiger, S. (2022). Cognitive behavioral therapy for daily life: A step-by-step guide to transforming your thoughts and habits. Rockridge Press.

Sinha, R. (2011). New findings on biological factors predicting addiction relapse vulnerability.

Current Psychiatry Reports, 13(5), 398–405. Retrieved from https://www.ncbi.nlm.nih.gov/pmc/articles/PMC3674771/

SMART Recovery. (n.d.). SMART Recovery. Retrieved from https://smartrecovery.org/

SMART Recovery. (2017). SMART Recovery facilitator's manual (2nd ed.). SMART Recovery. Retrieved from https://shop.smartrecovery.org/products/smart-recovery-facilitators-manual

SMART Recovery Training Center. (n.d.). GSF 203: Facilitator/Family & Friends Training. Retrieved from https://t2.smartrecoverytraining.org/moodle/mod/page/view.php?id=5728

Substance Abuse and Mental Health Services Administration. (2019). Enhancing motivation for change in substance use disorder treatment (Treatment Improvement Protocol (TIP) Series 35). Retrieved from https://store.samhsa.gov/product/TIP-35-Enhancing-Motiva

tion-for-Change-in-Substance-Use-Disorder-Treatment/PEP 19-02-01-003

Substance Abuse and Mental Health Services Administration. (2021). Enhancing recovery through peer support and self-help groups. U.S. Department of Health and Human Services. Retrieved from https://www.samhsa.gov

The Recovery Village. (n.d.). Why emotional intelligence is important in recovery. Retrieved from https://www.therecoveryvillage.com/recovery/wellness/emotional-intelligence-important-recovery

University of New Hampshire. (2023, March). Understanding the behavioral and neurobiological mechanisms of relapse in alcohol use disorder. Inquiry Journal. Retrieved from https://www.unh.edu/inquiryjournal/blog/2023/03/understanding-behavioral-neurobiological-mechanisms-relapse-alcohol-use-disorder

UpToDate. (n.d.). Substance use disorders: Motivational interviewing. Retrieved from https://www.uptodate.com/contents/substance-use-disorders-motivational-interviewing

U.S. Department of Health and Human Services, Substance Abuse and Mental Health Services Administration. (n.d.). National helpline: Free, confidential help. Retrieved from https://www.samhsa.gov/find-help/helplines/national-helpline

Volkow, N. D., Koob, G. F., & McLellan, A. T. (2016). Neurobiologic advances from the brain disease model of addiction. The New England Journal of Medicine, 374(4), 363–371. https://doi.org/10.1056/NEJMra1511480

Volkow, N. D., & Morales, M. (2015). The brain on drugs: From reward to addiction. Cell, 162(4), 712–725. https://doi.org/10.1016/j.cell.2015.07.046

Westbrook, D. (2016). Retrain your brain: Cognitive behavioral therapy in 7 weeks. Callisto Media.

West Virginia Department of Health and Human Resources. (2022). Evidence-based treatments for alcohol use disorder.Retrieved from https://dhhr.wv.gov/office-of-drug-control-policy/newsletters/Pages/Evidence-Based-Treatments-for-Alcohol-Use-Disorder.aspx

Yale Medicine. (2022, May 25). How an addicted brain works. Yale Medicine. Retrieved from https://www.yalemedicine.org/news/how-an-addicted-brain-works

Zhou, Y., Zhao, M., Zhou, C., & Li, R. (2016). Sex differences in drug addiction and response to exercise intervention: From human to animal studies. Frontiers in Neuroendocrinology, 40, 24–41. https://doi.org/10.1016/j.yfrne.2015.07.001